CW00820011

Let Me Say This
A Dolly Parton
Poetry Anthology

Julie E. Bloemeke & Dustin Brookshire
EDITORS

LAKE DALLAS, TEXAS

Copyright © 2023 edited by Julie E. Bloemeke & Dustin Brookshire
All rights reserved
Printed in the United States of America

FIRST EDITION

Requests for permission to reprint or reuse material from this work should be sent to:

Permissions
Madville Publishing
PO Box 358
Lake Dallas, TX 75065

Cover designed by Reid Strauss
Cover Photo © Dolly Parton 2020 by Fran Strine

Editors Julie E. Bloemeke and Dustin Brookshire are donating all annual royalties from *Let Me Say This: A Dolly Parton Poetry Anthology* to Dolly Parton's Imagination Library in honor of the Book Lady.

ISBN: 978-1-956440-51-5 paper, and 978-1-956440-52-2 ebook
Library of Congress Control Number: 2022949175

for Dolly Rebecca Parton

CONTENTS

TAKE ME BACK TO WHERE WE STARTED FROM

IT'S TIME I SHOW THE WORLD JUST WHAT I'M ABOUT

TRYIN' TO FIND WHAT FEELS LIKE HOME

READ INTO IT WHAT YOU WILL BUT SEE ME AS I AM

GUIDE ME AND KEEP ME

TAKE ME BACK TO WHERE WE STARTED FROM

A NOTE FROM EDITOR DUSTIN BROOKSHIRE

You're holding this anthology because you know it is full of damn good poems sharing in the Dolly love, praise, and tribute. I'm not saying that just because I had fifty percent of the say of what made it in here. It's the truth that you'll soon see for yourself.

Let me first tell you about my love of Dolly Parton, and why I'm the Dolly super fan that I am today—or as I like to say, a worshiper in the church of Saint Dolly Parton. Dolly is who I turn to when I need inspiration in general and especially when I need inspiration to believe in myself as a poet. Dolly graduated from Sevier County High School. Each graduate had to share from the stage what they were going to do with their lives. Dolly shared that she was moving to Nashville to become a star. The audience laughed. (Right!?! Who laughs at Dolly Rebecca Parton?) But the pain of that moment did not stop her; she left for Nashville the day after. Six years later, Dolly recorded *A Real Live Dolly* in her alma mater's gym, and likely performed in front of some of the same people who had laughed at her dreams at graduation. Dolly's tenacity to hold true to her ambitions—to shine amid and despite those that didn't support her—speaks to me as a gay man who has often felt like an outsider.

Dolly is even at the center of a 20+ year debate that I have with my best friend Chris Daughtrey. (No, not the *American Idol* singer.) The debate rages on even today. Chris won't concede that Dolly's cover of "Shine" is superior to the original version. He won't change his opinion, no matter how many times I remind him that Dolly's version is the Grammy winner.

Dolly has been there for me in so many crucial moments of my life. I'll admit it, it sounds dramatic, but it is true, and it is probably true for many of you as well. I was 19 and barely out as a gay man—with no one to confide in about my first heartbreak—when I cried to "Bargain Store" on repeat after my first boyfriend cheated on me. I knew Dolly understood. After I was raped in 2006, it was Dolly's music that comforted me when I was too ashamed to tell anyone. Dolly's music—pretty much every song I owned played on repeat—helped me move into a mental space where I could write about the rape, which enabled me to be in a space where I could receive therapy. "Light of a Clear Blue Morning" and "You Better Get to Livin'" were mantras on my long journey of healing. Years later, upon arriving home after eight exhausting hours of persuading a loved one to enter rehab, I discovered a copy of *Blue Smoke* waiting for me in my mailbox, courtesy of a friend in Australia. *Blue Smoke* wasn't scheduled for release in the US for a couple more months. I played the album, cried, and Dolly comforted me to sleep by track five, "Home." See what I'm saying? Dolly is always here for me.

In August 2011, I asked my good friend Julie E. Bloemeke to join me for Dolly's Alpharetta (GA) stop on her *Better Day* tour. We wore homemade shirts, pink scarves, and butterfly stickers on our cheeks. (We've provided evidence by way of our editor's photograph toward the end of this anthology.) We sang, danced, and cried. We were mesmerized. Then we did it all again in November 2016 when Julie joined me in Charleston (SC) for a stop on Dolly's *Pure & Simple* tour.

With our shared Dolly experiences, love, and enthusiasm, Julie was the person I needed to co-edit a special issue of my online poetry journal, *Limp Wrist*, to celebrate Dolly's 75th birthday in 2021. (Following this introduction is a nod to *Limp Wrist*'s Dolly issue with a poem by Denise Duhamel, Maureen Seaton, and Julie Marie Wade.) Julie and I had so much fun curating the issue that before we finished our work, the idea for a Dolly poetry anthology was percolating. Upon concluding our work for the special issue, immersed in Dolly adoration, we knew that we had to make a Dolly poetry anthology a reality. In a surprisingly quick twist of fate—Saint Dolly must have been looking out for us—we shared our idea with Kim Davis at Madville Publishing in December 2020 and here we are with *Let Me Say This: A Dolly Parton Poetry Anthology* celebrating its publication day on Dolly's 77th birthday.

If you're a diehard Dolly fan then you know—the title of the anthology's introduction section comes from "You're The Only One" and that *Let Me Say This* pays homage to Dolly's classic "Just Because I'm A Woman," from her 1968 album of the same name.

Dolly took "You're The Only One," written by Carole Bayer Sager and Bruce Roberts, to the number one spot on the country charts in 1979. *Take Me Back To Where We Started From* is a nod to the journey, from the labor of love in building the *Limp Wrist* special issue to *Let Me Say This*.

Dolly wrote "Just Because I'm A Woman" for her husband, Carl Dean. Eight months after they were married, Carl asked Dolly if she was a virgin when they got married. Carl got upset when Dolly answered the question honestly. A song was born, a message to both her husband and the music industry with its rampant double standards for men and women. Dolly believes that radio stations purposefully held back on playing her song, but it still became an anthem for women, and all us outsiders. I hope you'll give it a listen.

In closing, Julie and I are elated to share our What Would Dolly Do (WWDD) moment: each anthology purchased through Madville Publishing will raise money for Dolly Parton's Imagination Library because we're donating our annual royalties to the organization. I extend my deepest gratitude to everyone that submitted to the anthology, the contributors for allowing us to publish their poems, and you, for reading this anthology.

Denise Duhamel, Maureen Seaton & Julie Marie Wade

SEVENTY-FIVE LINES FOR DOLLY'S
SEVENTY-FIFTH

It costs me lots of money to look this cheap.
I've blown the budget on sequins before.
But I made a vow: I am not a sheep—

I am a shepherd writing songs galore,
once, two hit singles in a single day.
Yup, that was a good night, I said and swore

off Corona. Now I drink Beaujolais
and run lines for the *9 to 5* sequel.
I've got big dreams the boss can't take away—

can't *the man* see we ladies are equal?
I still carry a pistol in my purse,
but my grin's sincere, my heart's peaceful

as Baby Jesus in that Bible verse.
If I still had my many-colored coat,
I'd wrap it tight around the world, rehearse

as though the whole earth was my stage, then float
freely home to those Appalachian hills,
my beloved Smokies, where I co-wrote

"Rainbowland" with Miley Cyrus. Her skills
remind me of my own at twenty-four
when I touted Avon, and the cheap thrills

of cheap perfume traveling door-to-door.
I wrote "You Ask Me Not to Wear Cologne."
I wrote "Two Sides to Every Story"

with Porter before I went on my own.
After, I wrote "I Will Always Love You"
which you-know-who (Elvis) hoped to co-own.

No way, I said. Elvis stuck to his blue
Christmas, fever, and cold Kentucky rain,
and in the end, I kept that platinum tune.

I have big hair and a big business brain.
Long ago I turned those busty blonde jokes
on their busty blonde heads and broke the chain

on my ten-speed as I sped away, spokes
spinning like the 8-tracks of my first songs.
Then came my parade of wigs and dumb pokes

about my accent. Producers prolonged
my dependence on them. It took me years—
in fact, it almost took my life. What's wrong

with Romeos—songs that gave me my career—
or hit duets like "Islands in the Stream"?
We relied on each other, ah ha, steered

me to fame. Then Lily's and Jane's scheme
to make a women-in-the-workplace film
exploded in solidarity and team

play. The theme song was an anthem, a hymn
homage to heel-clicks and typewriter keys,
a companion piece for Abzug and Steinem

and all those sick of saying pretty please.
I've never called myself a feminist,
but I'll wear it if it means equality

for cowgirls, nurses, and receptionists.
I'm a Christian ally—no conflict there—
but I won't claim I'm fundamentalist

on any subject except footwear.
I once dubbed myself a "Backwoods Barbie"
and I'm okay with that. I'm debonair

on the inside. There's a yang you can't see
alongside my ultra-bedazzled yin,
or there's a jolt and an epiphany—

my ladylike boots are made of buckskin.
A cowboy in tight jeans might turn my head,
grab me to dance at Dollywood. Even

so, Carl's the only one who'll share my bed.
What's the secret to our 54 years?
Well, *You've got to know when to hold 'em*

like Kenny says. But we're all amateurs,
I've learned, and *ama* is the root of love,
all those Tennessean hoots and hollers.

My dark roots, split ends, push-up bras out of
style, second chances as snips and tucks—
everyone knows I'm neither blonde nor dumb.

You say you like my pipes. I say, *Aw, shucks.*
I sing what I feel, and I feel it deep—
my joie de vivre, puissance, and WTFs.

A NOTE FROM EDITOR JULIE E. BLOEMEKE

Dolly Parton's voice has a way of feeling like home. My Grandma Bette had a Southern inflection in her speech that was distinctly Dolly, complete with her own version of Dolly's pluck and humor. Even at five years old, I would crawl up into her lap, press my ear to her heart, dangle my legs off of the side of the chair and ask her to sing me to drowsy. And as she rocked me close, I was already hearing Dolly long before I knew who Dolly truly was.

The first Dolly song I remember memorizing was "The Seeker," but it was the film *9 to 5* that lassoed my absolute enchantment. Struck by her wit and wigs, her music and unabashed glitz, I saw Dolly's embodiment of presence as an invitation to truth: to own one's inimitable identity and self-expression. Dolly championed boundaries and jest, executing both with aplomb and a sense of what was right. Raised in Ohio, I was taught to *take no shit* as we say, and Dolly was a model not only for how not to take it, but also how to do one better: to rise above with a bevy of brains, a disarming turn of phrase, a dash of kindness, and a heap of cheek.

On August 4, 2011, I discovered Dolly had something more up her sequined sleeve. My long-time poet friend and fellow soul sister in shenanigans, Dustin Brookshire, asked me to join him for Dolly's *Better Day* tour in Alpharetta. We had spent many a late night driving in Atlanta, belting out Dolly tunes together. I had never seen Dolly in concert, and Dustin was determined to right my transgression. We schemed over outfits for months, and when the concert date arrived, we affixed glittering pink butterflies to our cheeks, threw sparkling magenta sashes over our shoulders, and strutted in wearing t-shirts Dustin had made for us: *Parton for President* for him, and *Parton Me* for myself. Somehow we remembered to ask a Dolly fan to snap a picture; it has since become our Dolly author photo, and it is our joy to share it with you as part of *Let Me Say This: A Dolly Parton Poetry Anthology*.

As the night went on—thick with epic Georgia humidity—I began to fall brazenly deeper into Dolly's allure. It was not just the affirmation of what we all already know—she is a masterful lyricist and musician, a brilliant storyteller and performer—it was that I came to discover the appeal of Dollyverse spirituality: Dolly does not preach about her relationship to God; she lives it—a truth she owns without reservation. There, amidst cowboy hats and fringe, glow bracelets and bustiers, was another bedazzled revelation: sexuality, sensuality, and spirituality were all inseparable and intertwined. For Dolly, and I realized for me too, part of *gettin' to livin'* was to embrace the self—divinely created—even if the rest of the rhinestone world thinks there is no place for hope, or kindness, or the sentimental.

And in that night of transcendence, Dustin held my hand. Neither of us could have fathomed that our love for Dolly would take us on a journey of co-editing a Dolly tribute issue of *Limp Wrist*, or that the mirth and awe of that experience would open the doors to this anthology, and to working with Kim Davis and the incomparable Madville Publishing team. Thank you, Kim, for raising your cup of ambition with us—and for embracing this project with such love and enthusiasm.

As a disciple of serendipity, I am hardly surprised to reveal this: 11 years to the day after we went to that first concert—because indeed there have been others—Dustin and I were editing on one of our many hours-long phone conferences, sifting through submissions for this anthology. Reading poems aloud to each other, marveling at work that stopped us in wonder and caused us to exclaim in glee, we both bore witness to the awe of how Dolly travels, transpires, and transforms. We hope you too will experience the synchronicity and magic that seem to follow Dolly in all she does, even in these pages.

Dustin and I agree that selecting final poems for this collection was one of the most challenging endeavors we have had to undertake; thank you to those who considered their work for this project. To see how beloved Dolly is, to see the range of ways in which she has impacted families and fans, was humbling—reverent even. For all of you that were generous enough to submit, we share our red shoes with you, and hope you keep on writing your *pretty rainbows brushed with love across the sky.*

In *Let Me Say This: A Dolly Parton Poetry Anthology*, we've gathered up a congregation of 54 poets who hold the diamond up to the light, shining facets of Dolly often overlooked or previously unconsidered. In these poems, we see Dolly reminding us to radically love ourselves just as we are—and amidst this, to emerge, to subvert, and to step into comedic timing with smarts, sass, savoir-faire, and spangle. We are so grateful to each poet in this collection for doing the seemingly impossible—making us all fall even more in love with Dolly.

I should mention that the danger in any tribute anthology is that it might become one note, but Dustin and I would like to think y'all kept the repertoire open—a little bluegrass, a little country, a bit of rock 'n' roll, a dash of rap, some yodelin'. And that maybe there's even a surprise pan flute a time or two.

We decided to divide the book into four parts, an arrangement intended to invite further conversation into Dolly's reach. For each section title we chose lyrics that elicited potential riffs between the song lines and the poems within:

In section one, we kick off with a bit from "Girl in the Movies": *It's Time I Show The World Just What I'm About.* Here Dolly awakens a sense of self in light of public and private persona; she reaches beyond the living room TV, the silver screen, the concert, the album, to remind us we aren't alone in our spiritual exploration or our heartbreak.

In *Tryin' To Find What Feels Like Home*, from "Travelin' Thru," an Academy Award and Golden Globe-nominated song written for the film *Transamerica*, poets navigate how Dolly defines and redefines a sense of home, both geographically and through our sense of self-perception and transformation. Dolly hearkens back to roots but also shows up across the US and overseas, calling in kin and road trips, oracles and crushes.

Read Into It What You Will, But See Me As I Am is from "Backwoods Barbie." An investigation into the relationship with the body, appearance, and societal roles, it is also the upending of gendered expectation, the embracing of the human fallible, and the championing of dress—or fashion expression—as gateway.

The last section of the book, *Guide Me And Keep Me*, from "The Seeker," speaks to expansion, the holding of a Dolly note a cappella, a reverberation into the ways we look to Dolly to appear in serendipity—how we invite her into our homes and hearts, into our families and our life milestones, how we turn to her for how to hold fast to the *dream no one can take away.*

We hope these poems little sparrow into your roots and your story, that they illuminate your divine sense of self, and elicit the magic and surprise of seeing Dolly in ways you had not previously envisioned. May they companion you in the clear blue morning of your contemplation, celebrate with you two doors down when you walk into a room looking like that; may they pray, subvert, talk back, and rise above. And may they raise praise for the great unifier, the queen of country, the Book

Lady, our angel of Appalachia, and our living saint of Tennessee. But most of all, may they keep you writing your own little heart out on the journey, remembering to stay kind, true, and just a little bit irreverent along the way.

*Maybe somethin' we've done might inspire people
to do a little better.*

—Dolly Parton

Dolly Parton's America, episode 9, "She's Alive"

IT'S TIME I SHOW THE WORLD

JUST WHAT I'M ABOUT

Chad Frame

THE INTIMATE BIOGRAPHY

Plumsteadville, Pennsylvania, 1990

Second grade, a trip to the library,
and the teacher tells us *go choose a book*

about a person who interests you.
Nothing interests an eight-year-old boy more

than attention. I snicker, swipe the slim
pink paperback I find hidden between

encyclopedias—*Dolly Parton:
The Intimate Biography*. We march

back across the cracked blacktop, up the ramp
to the modular classroom, to our seats.

Tomorrow you'll give a presentation,
she announces. I smirk, hiding my book,

dreaming of telling boob jokes to the class.
Then she adds, *while dressed up as the person*

you chose. Mortified, I remove the book
from my shirt. My hand shoots up. *Please*, I beg,

can I pick someone else? My teacher's name
is lost to time, but I still remember

her pitiless face—*You had time to choose.*
That night, I ask my mother to take me

to our rural town's only grocery
store, buy supplies, then study my pink book.

The next morning, presidents, astronauts,
football heroes, and one eight-year-old boy

wearing a mop head, inflated balloons
stuffed up his shirt, are paraded onstage

with the entire school watching from the seats.
And somehow, instead of what I prepared,

the words to a song come to me, high-voiced
and quavering, sang to the assembly—

So, with patches on my britches, and holes
in both my shoes, in my coat of many

colors, I hurry off to school—to find
the others laughing, making fun of me.

I wish I could tell you this story ends
with applause. I know you know it doesn't.

THE GREAT EQUALIZER

is a house party, vodka-soaked, stuffed sneaker-to-sneaker on the back porch, smoke shouting out our open mouths. Between the nearby leaves, the bod-hot dark cuts into equal parts like a Devil's Food Cake while inside bodies thick-glide like icing on another's hips, decadent magic, mastering the reverent tremble in our hands.

When somebody tossed Dolly Parton in rotation, somewhere between afrobeats and my best friend bussin' like we practiced in the floor-length back home, I thought it was a joke.

Picture it: black kids turned bright bell of laughter. We pealed from the shadows, hee-hawing and hollering like we stumbled in the wrong bar but ain't scared, and we been there, looking for ghosts between barstools and dust

praying for a stranger's familiar face to emerge from the bathroom or the front door, someone to remind us we aren't the only ones left in the world to wound

but I've been bad about looking at the bigger picture—my whole crew held like a deep breath in the old-school sepia of a single lamp,

waiting. Room thrummin' with guitar swang and the boot-dug twang of mourning—*Joleeeeene* Dolly pleads and we damp, tremblin', ready to moan—*Jolene, Jolene, Joleeeeene—*

what do we know about heartbreak that ain't in our marrow already?

Kari Gunter-Seymour

PERFECT PITCH

I rode middle school-bound
in the back seat of my aunt's station wagon,
listening to her and mama sing "Jolene,"
trading verses, harmonizing the chorus,
I'm begging of you please don't take my man!

A few years later it was "9 to 5."
They were fired up and it was Dolly's doing.
This was rural Ohio, the bottom lip
of Northern Appalachia,
right shy of Perry Como country.

The women in the family worked
the TS Trim factory, spitting out
Honda car parts. Started out
on the assembly line, worked their way up
to paint, then detailing, then welding.

The physical labor made their bodies strong,
their future bright and like Dolly,
they weren't taking any shit.
They learned early on about strikes and picket lines,
how important it was to organize and vote.

Brave women in the work force, determined
to see their daughters inside college classrooms,
the hell out of factory row.
I didn't know then that I was being raised
by a feminist, taking back her power.

Like Dolly, my mama would never use that word,
no matter how much she embodied it.
She was proud to hang up her welder's helmet
end of shift, pick up her paycheck, sing in the front seat
of a station wagon with women she loved.

Dorianne Laux

DOLLY SAID "NO" TO ELVIS

Dolly said *no* to Elvis and waited for Whitney.
She didn't know she was waiting, she just kept
writing and singing. Elvis wanted to cover it,
and Dolly was thrilled, but he also wanted a share
of the publishing rights. Dolly said *no* and cried
all night, loving Elvis of the swiveling hips
and flop of dark hair, his high baritone voice
that could cover two octaves and a third,
nothing like her light bright soprano.
Dolly, never to be outdone, could cover five.
Beat that Mr. Pelvis! But like any King he wanted
his gold and Dolly, a poor girl with a big family,
wanted to leave her songs to them.
And she didn't know she was waiting for Kevin
Costner who suggested Whitney sing it
for *The Bodyguard*, insisted on the a cappella intro.
When Dolly first heard it she pulled off the road,
turned up the radio, marveled at how Whitney
took her simple song and made it *a mighty thing,*
beautiful Whitney who also covered five octaves
with her perfect vibrato. And though
both Elvis and Whitney died early,
Dolly lives on, her voice unchanged by age, lilting
across the stage at 74, her life far from over, still
singing and singing and singing. A mighty little thing.

Katie Manning

DOLLY, WHEN I MET YOU THERE WAS PEACE

Your songs were my earliest islands.
I learned to set a small needle gently in
between black vessels, to sail away on the
intertwined voices and leave the stream
of sadness behind. Then there was that
summer my sisters and I watched (no, that is
not the word) *belted* along with you what
we heard from the screen each day when we
alternated *Rhinestone Cowboy*
with *Mary Poppins.*
Between
then and now, you've been almost perfect:
you mail books to millions of kids,
denounce racism with a smile (*Do we
think our little white asses
are the only ones that matter?*),
how you can also be
my island, a place where I can't be wrong
and everything is nothing for a while. I still sail
with you sometimes when I need to get away,
back to my grandparents' house, back with
that record player, back, somehow, to me.

Tyler Gillespie

DOLLY PARTON ARGUES A THEORY OF LINGUISTICS. POSITS

Dolly Parton argues   a theory of linguistics. Posits
we construct identities   through words

& *just because I'm blonde   don't think I'm dumb.*

Saussure, however, might disagree.   Claims language
is arbitrary.   The relationship between Signifiers
& Signified is socially encoded.   Relies on difference.

We define words   (concepts)   by what they are not.

This rationale of difference   then extends to people
as we construct identities   through words.

Parton   of course   is one of our greatest philosophers,
often cited for   her 9-to-5 treatise on capitalism.

I admire her dedication to working   class struggles,

but it's her embrace   of difference I find most radical.
The way we see both ourselves   & each other in her words.

L.J. Sysko

THE YASSIFICATION OF DOLLY PARTON

Even from behind a counter
under a caul of flaming hair
Jolene must've seen how a harrier carries her call

tree to mountain   hoists whole the holler
teasing it high   or how heaven

loans a magpie one single sequin at a time

how a warbler whistles beside snow-melt slide
until her heart   a hunter
wheels in exercise   how a hawk

casts her shadow   behind peacock disguise
Oh   little mouse   listen—

you're from Barefoot Rise   below Rib-Thin

hunkered under a tinsel umbrella
humming the tune   of spangled sky
gamboling brookside   A steel on silver strings

you tremble   Spread wide   wings sound
loud as the first time

you heard there was such a thing as song

Let her lift
your longing   pretty
until you forget you

alone can't float   flee   fly
Dolly!

Dive!   Swipe want from a meadow   pince its warm hide

Roll   peck   break   blind
This bank where desire mole-holes to survive
          Hold   It   Up

Write a note then push it   reaaaal   slowww
acrylics scraping through

a window in time

Here   beautiful
                    RUN

                                        my lines

Linda Neal Reising

DOLLY'S DEBUT

My mother would pop the corn we had grown
in the garden, reward for our summer thumbs,
sore after shelling, separating pearl-like kernels
from cob. Daddy would bring home a six-pack
of Grapette, glass bottles rattling inside
the cardboard carrier. These nights, we splurged,
split two bottles four ways, then clustered
around the television set, a nearly-new Zenith
color console, Christmas surprise my parents
paid out on time. That September Tuesday night,
we were prepping for *The Porter Wagoner Show*,
my father's favorite, although he still mourned
the leaving of Norma Jean, as if she were dead
instead of quitting to marry. At twelve, I rolled
my eyes at Speck Rhodes, the Wagonmasters,
the corny barn backdrop, the flashy suits,
the pompadours. But that night in '67,
when Porter introduced the *little gal* named
Dolly Parton, clad in her sleeveless red dress
with garnet brooch, sporting a platinum bouffant,
I sat up straight as she flashed her dimples
and began to wail "Dumb Blonde." Still buck-toothed,
pudgy, my braids as lifeless as sunning black snakes,
I dreamt of being her, believed that a plain
girl from the Ozark foothills could be remade
into a star, a nova, if only she believed.

Rupert Fike

THE PORTER WAGONER SHOW

My father always calling him, *Ole Porter,*
          Saturday afternoons
around our mammoth yet fuzzy Zenith,
         Granny's doily on top,
the aunts in their chairs, me on the hassock,
suddenly interested in country music
         since the Beatles did that Buck Owens song.
Rhinestone suits and corn pone jokes—
         my introduction to camp—
the aunts lapping it up, their world irony-free.
         They'd sifted Martha White,
         used a crank telephone,
         grown up in east Tennessee.
They laughed at Lonzo, adored String Bean.
Porter's weekly gospel song becoming a favorite when
         The New Girl, (what we all called her)
showed up to sing hymns like she meant it.
         That one's just being herself, Granny said.
The Zenith pixels responding, their lines stacked
         tighter now, cathode rays shooting straighter
         when we heard the words,
         And now, Dolly.
This became my sign to scoot the hassock closer,
         lean, touch the rabbit ears,
         her cowgirl blouse sharpening,
         its mother-of-pearl buttons straining,
         heroic in their effort,
         reflecting studio lights,
The New Girl flowing through me now.
Oh, blessed contrast! Oh, genuine smile! Oh, buttons!
         And no matter how stretched or cramped
         my loving arms got, when my father yelled,
         There! Hold it right there, son,
I was to freeze, remain her antenna while she sang,
         an intimacy I held dear—

it was just between us.
Plus my father had called me *son*.
Maybe she'd sing two this week.
Papa loved that hymn, Aunt Dora sniffed.
Sally! My father yelled back to Mama
in the kitchen.
Sally, quick! Ole Porter's got the new girl on again!

Beth Gylys

BREAKUP

He couldn't own the core of who you are
although he tried to keep you in his net,
take all the credit for your rising star.

His *pretty little thing*, you'd strum guitar
and belt out songs beside him. Your voices met
and blurred: songs, the witness of who you are,

were pouring out of you back then. Demure
you stand beside him with downcast eyes on set.
You knew you had to leave—your rising star

just coming into view—his arm a tether
and a weight. You smile. You loved him, yet
you wouldn't cede the core of who you are.

You wrote "I'll Always Love You," the words like fire
tore through you as he listened, heard. You'd get
your freedom with his tears. You, risen star,

forgave lawsuit, slander…paid off his debts, and more,
held hands and sang to Porter on his deathbed.
I'll never be that good, Dolly. You are
beyond me: a living saint, a guiding star.

Yvonne Zipter

TOO MUCH FOR ME

I was a teenager in a house that might've felt familiar
to a Hawthorne's Hester Prynne when Dolly Parton first
walked into our tidy living room. My stepfather became lord
of the television every Saturday night, and for three hours

we'd leave Milwaukee for the country via *Hee Haw*,
the Wilburn Brothers, and Porter Wagoner and their shows.
And there, next to Porter, with his sequined suit coats,
his hair slick as a sixties T-Bird logo, was Dolly, her bosom

threatening to break free from of its ruffled prison
and strike out on its own, her hair the size of Ohio
and fluffy as carnival cotton candy. They'd stand
beside a rustic railing or maybe a sage-green barn,

a single microphone between them as if that's all
they could afford, warbling songs of love and infidelity,
poverty and moonshine, while my own tastes ran to Layla
and Lola and black magic women. When Dolly sang solo,

a guitar strapped across her shoulder, her right breast
took a rest in the curve of its voluptuous wooden body.
I was a teenaged girl on the verge of coming out,
and Dolly was, quite simply, too much woman for me.

Phillip Watts Brown

IF YOU PLAY "JOLENE" AT 33 RPM

Dolly's vocals lower
to a cowboy croon:

I'm begging of you   please
don't take my man.

Slow any song
and sorrow blooms

like blood
through a bandage.

Slow sorrow
and it darkens like dusk—

stained windows.
Outside, moths fire-dance

around a porch light,
a black horse breathes

in a field, lungs filling
with night.

The words curve
into prayer: *please*

don't take him
even though you can.

Jolene as Jesus
green-eyed with fiery hair,

the god
gay men at bedsides begged

to spare their loves.
Imagine the quiet

when she didn't answer.
Sound of the stylus lifted,

the record still turning.

Julie E. Bloemeke

DOLLY WOULD

It's too easy to Pigeon Forge Dolly
into *9 to 5*, DD twang, to not heed
her *Better Day* concert advice: *Darlin',*

own your truth. Because Dolly became
Dolly in a fallen chapel of deep woods
Tennessee, strumming into the air,

praising into the only tongue
she knew, her congregation of God,
song, and sex—naked graffiti lusting

sanctuary over the walls: *The sexuality,*
the spirituality, the sensuality, that's exactly
who I am, she tells *Dolly Parton's America,*

the joy of the truth I found there is with me
to this day. I had found God and I found
Dolly Parton and I loved them both.

And don't forget how they all tried
to stop her, but even Daddy *couldn'ta*
wooped the glitter outta her, as she snuck

out back to press pokeberries to her lips,
line her eyes with blackened match tips,
or how she'd head over to town

just to witness some somethin' somethin'
strutting down the walk, goldfish swimming
in those coveted acrylic heels, an invocation

for this woman's *town trollope* red nails,
breasts booming forward, all a beyond
compare to the eventual Jolene. And all

the mothers saw this too, said, *oh no,*
ducking their heads, checking
that top button for good measure,

already forming the trash words
they would whisper later over fences.
I admit it: I too used to see only wigs

and corsets until I finally got it: only
so much fake could be true.
And tonight Dolly proves it, pulls in

the lights all around her, invites us
to pour into that same cup of ambition,
all 5 foot something of her who yodels,

fiddles, plays bluegrass, raps then can't,
belts gospel, all a capella in her little sparrow,
louder than a thunderstorm, sending chills

through 98 degrees of solid humidity,
whooping us still under cowboy hats,
all the faces painted just like hers

smiling back from their derelict hearts
into a song of every last thing unsaid.
A woman married decades who writes

heartbreak like she's lost every last time,
this country blood in all of her colors, shakes
herself to fire in rhinestone fringe, opens

the butterfly down in me, holds the mic
to the voice I never allowed, says,
own your trash, says *make a joyful*

noise, says *I've always been,* says, *Jesus.*
And I want to tell her how my shut
mouth was my loaded gun, my quiet khaki

was a way to hide; I was taught never
to be noticed, learned that my peace kept
my father's hands from raising, my mother's

voice from breaking, that the good girl
took almost 40 years to realize she wasn't,
and good wasn't best besides. I am not my own

island in this stream, but now together you and I,
Dolly, we sparkle and quake, we are holding
everything, walking down that same city street,

the higher the hair the closer to God, singing
mighty after mighty fractured song,
stomping our glitz & sex & Jesus,

praising with every last step,
and here we come again.
God. And there I go.

Kelli Russell Agodon

WERE IT NOT FOR THE MOONLIGHT

for the I've-never-been-to-Dollywood
eyeshadow, an eyebrow pencil and a sense

of style—Truvy's Cuppa Cuppa Cuppa Cake,
it might rain fruit cocktail or a sackful

of appreciation for fruit cocktail because
we were so thankful for Dolly to play God

on *Grace and Frankie*, ready for goodness
in the world to hold a Jolene cocktail

of sweet tea vodka, peach schnapps,
and cheer the minty Dolly like someone

muddling the world and taking what we love
to making mojitos, singing, "Here you come again"

as the drag queens dress in their large blonde wigs
and lip sync in cowgirl boots while I re-pencil

my eyebrows, add a little extra mascara
because we're all a little tipsy and dare to be

beautiful, all of us who love icons, who smile
and stumble, slow dancing with the moon.

SPIRIT OF '76

Seventy-six trombones aren't pert near enough
brass instruments to celebrate Dolly's 76th birthday.
Not even if they were led in formation by Professor
Harold Hill himself draped in a coat of many colors.
Everybody knows what happens when you hitch your
star to a Porter Wagoner. When a so-called "Dumb

Blonde" shines like the sun, but so much brighter
and she's the "Star of the Show." What choice did
Dolly have but to soar like an eagle? Transcending
Nashville and Motown, Hollywood and Broadway,
Greenwich Village and Laurel Canyon. Earthbound
Honky-Tonk Angel with her eyes on the sparrow,

fingers on the frets of a blue guitar, and enough wigs
to make every *RuPaul's Drag Race* queen green with
envy. Arriving in a white "limozeen," to save the world
with a trunkful of vaccines, an abundance of books to fill
the shelves of the library of your kid dreams. Reassuring
anyone within earshot that she will always love us.

Carolyn Oliver

I OVERHEAR A BOY HUMMING "JOLENE" WHILE HE PRACTICES LONG DIVISION

and, sudden as a train's blue note
—I know I don't deserve it—
Dolly Parton becomes the president.

The West Wing's garlanded in rhinestones, fringed
in bushels of Tennessee River pearls
while ambassadors wait on their whiskeys

because Dolly's out in the Rose Garden
serenading troublemaker nuns and poll workers,
sunbathing marchers who need a rest,

and later there'll be weddings on the portico
while sparrows feast on cornmeal flung
by drag queens shimmering in always golden-hour light.

In research labs they're whistling, they're twirling
their pipettes because there's banana pudding
in the fridge, and they know Dolly's working too:

today she's sending picture books and wheelchairs
and antiretrovirals all across the heartland
and into every city, today she's unraveling

acres of lace to wrap up every shivering mother,
today she's going to call us *darling*
and we will believe, really believe, we are cherished—

and no, not even the miracle of Dolly
can sway the wildfires, not even
her limpid soprano can dredge all rivers,

but let me tell you, since Dolly Parton became the president,
strawberries taste right again
and they're ripe all year long.

Donna Vorreyer

DOLLY REFUSES THE NOMINATION

There are no rules for rock and roll,
no one to say that her rhinestone repertoire,
honed through years and sweat,
is not a proper definition.

Having crooned and burned
and stepped out from shadows
that only women see, she knows
that melody and lyric, no matter

the backbeat, can rock the senses
and roll the stone from the tomb.
Seventy-six years behind her, flooding
the Opry with angelic trills and plaintive ballads,

and you want to honor her now
for being a rocker? She is so many things—
glamour and glory, backwoods and banter,
storyteller and songbird, magnolia blooming

from Little Pigeon roots. She will not give herself
this new label, though songs swim in her dreams
and wake in her fingers, music her heartbeat,
a small fist in her chest shaking a tambourine.

Arden Levine

IF THIS SONG SEEMS STRANGE, IT'S JUST BECAUSE I DON'T KNOW HOW TO PRAY.

To me, it's a bluegrass song as soon as you take out the piano.
—Dolly Parton, on her cover of Billy Joel's "Travelin' Prayer"

1.
I think New Yorkers are supposed to be cool
with Billy Joel. To me, though, he's an ex-
boyfriend, an ex-husband, an ex-geography

further out on the island where I live (but far
enough out that they give it a different name
and identity, and you sing about leaving it).

2.
When Billy asks *Hey Lord, won't ya look out
for her tonight?*, he is putting in a request.
When Dolly asks *Hey Lord, won't ya look out*

for him tonight?, she's cashing in a favor that
she knows she's probably owed. Billy is new
at this. Dolly is picking up the regular route.

3.
I'm in the car and B is driving and A is playing
tunes they will feature in their wedding,
sun melting a sweet knife-spread of highway.

Me: *Dolly covers this?* B: *Covers what?*
Me: *This is a Billy Joel song.* B: *It's a
Dolly Parton song. I don't care who wrote it.*

4.
A song is a location. Sometimes a song is New
York, sometimes Tennessee, sometimes all
points between a *now, here* and a *once, there*.

Billy starts the song with a locomotive piano
and Dolly starts it with a rail-rider's fiddle,
but, Lord, they both just want love to come home.

5.
C sings the song live at A and B's wedding and
her big Dolly voice fills the Brooklyn hall with
so much breath that our hearts float to the ceiling.

But, here's the kick: Her little baby, just born
and held to her chest, stays asleep the whole time.
Find where my baby's gonna be. Right here, mama.

6.
Dad, I stand over your grave but I don't know
where you are. A poem is a location but we can't
be found somehow. *Hey Lord, if you ever find*

the time, won't you tell him I miss him every day?
I needed Dolly to make it about me looking
for you. You stopped looking and then stopped.

7.
Lord, A and B are so goddamned happy and
I love them so much and they will never be
lost from each other. I should mention that

I married them, this bassist and pianist, held
their hands when they presented their vows,
strings holding keys, everything flying open.

8.
I wasn't raised in the church. I wasn't raised
with any faith. *Hey Lord, won't ya look out*
for him tonight, for he is far away from me?

This poem seems strange. Billy, I don't know
how to pray, either. Maybe Dolly can teach
us both. Love is a location. Oh Lord, Dad,

I'm right here.

TRYIN' TO FIND WHAT FEELS LIKE HOME

Nicky Beer

DRAG DAY AT DOLLYWOOD

... some of them look more like me than I do.
—Dolly Parton

Blue beehives whirl and loopily ascend
long paper wands. Candied apples smash into
shades of Vixen, Strike Me Pink, Cherries in the Snow.
Lamé by the square mile ripples under the Tennessee sun.
From a distance, the Mountain Sidewinder looks like a drunk,
bejeweled caterpillar. The screams sound the same as on any other day.
By closing time, seven hundred and eighty-two press-on nails
will have been lost. A few contrarians bust out their best
Patsys or Lorettas, dark bouffants stippling
the deluge of blonde. Someone's great-aunt
comes as Kenny Rogers and strokes her beard
like a newly-adopted lapdog. A bus from Atlanta
unleashes two dozen Dollys in matching bowling jackets,
Gutter Queens sprawled across their backs in lilac script.
To relieve the boredom at the Mystery Mine line,
someone hollers *When I say 'Homo' you say 'Sapiens.'*
Homo! SAPIENS! Homo! SAPIENS!
Dollys line the perimeter of the bald eagle sanctuary,
watching the raptors swoop stoically on the other side
of the netted enclosure. *They mate for life!* Dolly exclaims,
reading from Wikipedia on her phone. *Awww,* Dolly says.
Ughhh, says Dolly. A tall Dolly gives a short Dolly
a piggyback ride through Jukebox Junction, making
a laughing, lumbering chimera of poly satin and fringe.
Dolly holds back Dolly's hair as she vomits purple
slush and kettle corn into a bank of azaleas.
Dolly, with weary patience, explains to Dolly
why she can't pet her service dog. Dollys grasp
turkey legs in their fists, tear flesh from bone.
Thousands of pairs of Dolly lungs breathe in
gasoline and grease, breathe out glitter. Dolly

visits the restroom to check her wig and loses
track of herself in the mirrors. Dolly drifts
along an automated river, an undiagnosed tumor
humming gently under her lifejacket. Dolly
holds a thumb and forefinger up to the setting sun,
pinches it, and lovingly places it in Dolly's back pocket.
Dolly, exhausted and sunburned, collapses
onto a bench, rests her head on Dolly's breast,
who rests her head on Dolly's breast, who rests
her head on Dolly's breast on Dolly's breast.

Dan Vera

PILGRIMAGE

Here we go again,
another December,
another endless drive
through leafless Tennessee,
my gay husband and dog
on our yearly pilgrimage
to family awaiting us in Dallas.
When her bouffant smiles
from a billboard outside of Bristol:
her park in holiday splendor
lies a hundred miles ahead.
So we drive on through Knoxville,
sing "Jolene" to one another,
hum "Islands In the Stream"
as she repeatedly appears
with enticements to wonder
about its "festive parade," and
her "Smoky Mountain Christmas."
By the time we reach the turnoff
we have made up our minds
to extend our lengthy drive,
to stop and remind ourselves
of what has always brought us joy.
In Sevierville, Dolly's image cast in bronze.
Shoeless, she sits perched on a boulder,
holding tight to a guitar, with her face
frozen in happiness as if at just being alive.
We are two boys grinning,
gazing at her image and grateful
for her example, open-hearted,
unapologetic, a fearless
self-possession in her lifetime
made out of song.

Lana K. W. Austin

DOLLY KEEPS ON BURNIN'

You could say it's because we're practically kin,
me from Kentucky and her from Tennessee, both
born in dark hollers that still had joy despite the hardship,
both of us climbing out of the void with our voices.
But I see so much more than that. All you have
to do is watch for five seconds, whether she's singing,
speaking, or just sitting there, and you can see it, too,
the burning: a light, a flame, stars twinkling, whole galaxies
coming into existence, with mammoth suns so big
they make ours look like a teensy green bean
you snap on the front porch with your granny,
aunts, and cousins. Then come the subtler times,
how she gently embers herself, a tender candle flicker
or part of the soft reds of late-night campfires,
how the color becomes a gentle pulse pushing out
and into us in the middle of the night, with a thrum,
heartbeat of heat, of life, but muted now, magic
in the music, even in the quiet. That's still Dolly
with her light then, too, her music kissing our skin until
it starts to burn down deeper and reaches our bones,
where the hurt's real bad, but the love's real good,
too. Yes, Dolly's down bone-deep with us and knows
what matters, every hard-won truth blazing
a celestial trail. It's the torch she lights in every song
she sings and in everything she does, it's her endless
shimmer, always glowing, glowing, and glowing.

Rachel Morgan

THESE MOUNTAINS

You might tell yourself you want to leave, and you do—
you leave, in your twenties for a coast, for a man,

the next decades you visit the sagging porch, Dad's cough,
red-spotted salamanders, muddy oracles of the mountain.

Your grandfather taught you which grapevines to swing,
how to brew mountain tea, tie string to a June bug's leg.

He's memory now, visits as dappled sun through trees,
porch swings, a laugh that rumbles and cracks.

In the kitchen, Dolly's song "My Tennessee Mountain Home"
blisses from the speakers. Its earnestness catches

you off guard. Your therapist says we remember more
bad things than good, to protect our future selves.

Your lyric-filled heart, heavy on the vine, sodden with
experience, is suddenly blithe. The July ditches wave

with orange lilies, each their own little sun orbiting
eloquent stems as cars eclipse. It happens now, a moment

poofs to memory—to dwell on something becomes a dwelling,
constantly constructing the cabin where you lived and live.

Jennifer Wheelock

LESSON TWO

God's Country. That's what my mom called
East Tennessee. If I questioned why
this corner of our state was more heavenly
than other places, she declared:
the Great Smoky Mountains, green hills,
four distinct seasons, and Dolly Parton.
I only ever wanted to leave, longed
for any coast, saw the sea as a promise
of something bigger on the other side.
Some Sundays after church and fried chicken
we drove the 30 minutes to Sevierville to slow roll
past Dolly's old home. Pine needles danced
on the car hood, the roads were narrow,
and the windshield wipers whined.
In front of the rickety cabin, I imagined
Dolly on the front porch, envied
that she sang herself out of there. Maybe
that's why she still can sing tenderly about it,
the way I learned to love you because I left.

Stephen Roger Powers

CLEOPARTON

Not all eyes are on Dolly
when ten muscle-bound men in gold
loincloths carry her litter with asp arm

rests through Dollywood. White linen
with a jeweled shawl and ochre stenciled in
diamond bites on her cheek draw card
riffle shutter clicks. A fan of blue

ostrich feathers commands her gleaming men
to move faster. Halfway out the exit gate
a boy squeezes in, hand up, and Dolly leans

down, beads in her straight Egyptian
hair swinging, for a quick, careful palm press.

Nicole Tallman

DOLLY STYLE

I went to Tennessee
but skipped out on Dollywood.
I tend to avoid doing what I'm told,
like working a 9-to-5 job, having kids,
marrying a man. No thank you.
What's the appeal in doing
what everyone says we should?
When a well-meaning local said,
You can't come to Pigeon Forge without seeing Dollywood,
I hightailed it straight to Memphis.
Cranked "Jolene" the whole drive there.
I think Dolly would approve.
And when I got to Memphis
I skipped out on Graceland too.

Raye Hendrix

EUGENE, OREGON/HOMESICK

The year bleeding its dark half
backwards into summer, autumn
sweeping in like ink fanning
clear water, morning suddenly
cold against the glass.

Something unfamiliar sticking
to the trees—dew? Sap? Day
slips into a small handful
of illuminated hours.

No lightning bugs to pepper
night with living stars,
no stars, hardly even a moon,
the sky blanched by the city's
bright haze.

No cicadas. No choir of insects
to sing me to sleep, nothing
like home—Alabama—its wet
heat like the soft breath after
a kiss—

But Dolly said the people
here were kind, so kind
she wrote a song about them—
and I want to believe her.
I want to love this place.
I don't think Dolly would lie.

Isaiah Vianese

MY BROADWAY CRUSH COVERS
"WILDFLOWERS"

Decades after Dolly's recording for *Trio*,
he makes his own way, and I'm drawn
into the sweetness of his tenor.
I've long moved from my hometown.
Now, boys in New York call me
beautiful and *babe*,
hold my hand while we walk
under the lights of 42nd Street.
I often forget the quiet grass of my childhood
until a tune like this
marks the distance between now and then.
That kid is long gone,
and I rarely miss his loneliness.

Tonight as my crush kissed me at 48th and 9th,
pink blossoms fell from the sky.
Then we drank wine and talked for hours.
I rode the train home,
listening to "Wildflowers" again.
I thought about Dolly writing the song
and how she may not have known
what it would mean for queer men like us,
how such music carried us to the city
where we could finally grow.

Jeffrey Perkins

NASHVILLE

Sometimes I wonder what it might feel like
to live just outside town

in a house where folks keep night up too late
and I'd write you a song

and lay out our lives in chorus and verse—
call up our living in a simple way.

But I've never picked up a guitar. Never felt
its smooth neck in my arms

or felt the tension go out of its strings like
the slow chill of a summer's end.

I've heard it's having a revival resting
on its wide river and it's time to go.

Sometimes, I think how it might be to buy
that spot out of town with the money

I saved—anyone could stay the night.
And you'd look over one night like Dolly's

song I sing inside, imagining I wrote it
for you, *take me back to where we started from.*

Jeffrey Perkins

SAN FERNANDO

Here you come again in the slightest swimsuit
you could find, flexing and sunning your body
in the light like there's no care in the world
and I can feel your glow 3,000 miles away.

Like an earthquake in San Fernando earlier today.
Just enough to move someone's day. They say
the big one is on its way. We're living in a shadow
of something we can't see coming.

You're swimming in a pool taking selfies
at an evening's end—*looking better than a body
has a right to*—and I'm here watching your future
memories—imagining what comes after night falls.

And there was an earthquake in San Fernando
earlier today. Just enough to move someone's day.
They say the big one is on its way. We're living
in a shadow of something we can't see coming.

*All you gotta do is smile that smile and there go
all my defenses.* The last photo in the house of
you, dressed up and nowhere to go. You look
ready for an opening you can't see coming.

Here you come again. Just enough to move my day.
The big one is on its way so I'm living in a shadow
of something I can't see coming. Shaking me up.
Just when I'm about to make it work without you.

Dustin Brookshire

DOLLY AT THE FOX THEATER (2008)

My mother glanced at my shirt
as we waited, said,
I don't know why you wore
a Dairy Queen shirt to see Dolly?
I laughed, told her to look again.

My shirt says Dolly Queen.
She looked away like
something else caught her eye.
The tour bus door swung open,
a redhead exited first.
It's Dolly's best friend, Judy,
I whispered. Dolly waved
as she walked down the bus steps,
pausing at the bottom to listen
to what we, her fans, were yelling.

Early in the show, Dolly asked
if there were any drag queens
in the audience. My mother fidgeted
in her seat. Someone near
the front row jumped to her feet.
Well, usually the drag queens
come dressed as me, Dolly laughed
before launching into "Jolene."
When she sang the chorus
for the second time,
she crooned, *drag queen, drag queen,*
drag queeeeen. Please don't take my man.
The crowd cheered.
I screamed *Yaaaaaas.*
My mother looked to her lap.

Seated with an autoharp,
Dolly told us about her coat of many colors,

and love for her mother. She asked
if there were mothers in the audience,
a few yelled,
several hands shot up,
including my mother's.
Well, I dedicate this song
to all the good mommas out there.
I placed my arm around my mother,
squeezed her tight, leaned my head
against hers, gave her that moment.

Caridad Moro-Gronlier

NEVER DID SAY SO

After Dolly Parton's "To Daddy"

We jumped a red-eye to France to celebrate
a decade of marriage, and I prayed
to love him as much as I loved Paris.

I willed myself to shine like the Seine
through the clock at the Orsay, to stop
at least once a day and kiss him

along the Champs-Élysées. I willed my body
to unfurl like an accordion in his hands,
to murmur & bellow the song of Le Marais,

but no matter how I unreeled the filmstrip
of the we I willed us to be, his face remained
obscured in every image, the lens trained on me.

Not that I said so in a language he understood.
I walked ahead and switched to French when we deplaned,
rendered him mute with sentences

he didn't ask me to translate—
Sil vous plait, pouvez-vous nous aider?
Nous sommes perdus.

He believed I was fluent enough to speak
for both of us and didn't think to learn
any words for himself.

Content to nod and follow,
he didn't blame me when I got us lost
on the way to our last dinner

on the Rue de Soleil because the driver
heard Rue Désolée and drove the wrong way
across town, a mistake that encapsulated our lives—

the two of us stuck in a moving vehicle, miles
between sunny and sorry, an error that tripled
our fare and cost far more than we'd planned for.

I apologized, but he laughed because France
still ran on Francs and he still had enough
patience to forgive me anything. I nodded

when the driver offered to appease us
with *un peu de musique américain* and slid
Dolly Parton's Greatest Hits into the cassette deck.

My husband took my hand then, confessed
how relieved he was to know the words,
how happy he was to be going home.

Such a good omen, he said, but he was mistaken.
No omen was Dolly, but an oracle, a prophesy
singing about the fate of a woman who never did tell

of what she felt, who faked her grin and forgot
her face, who willed herself to love the noose
of her wedding ring. The last verse told everything

she never said—how her longing was vaster than silence,
how she bolted the door behind her,
how she never did say goodbye.

READ INTO IT WHAT YOU WILL

BUT SEE ME AS I AM

HOW DO YOU, AS A WOMAN, DARE
TO WRITE ABOUT SEX?

I don't want to talk about it—the men who think I'm some kind of skank. The grad school advisor who closed his office door and whispered that he was fantasizing about me, then asked, Was I doing the same? The other professor who just *knew* all my poems were about him. The editor who wrote: *I could use one of your orgasms today.* The other editor who sent me his phone number, address, and blurry photo of what might have been his cock. *Maybe I should stop*, I said. But David Lehman shook his head, *Men are disgusting. Don't let them inhibit or silence you, Nin.* I was relieved to find out that Denise Duhamel received weird notes after writing *The Woman with Two Vaginas. I love vaginas, too*, one fan said. She told me creepy stories about other women-poets who dared to write about sex. And I told her about the guy who called from a truck stop on I-95. He said he was going to be driving by my hometown of Poland, Ohio, just passing through en route to Chicago, and wanted to stop by and meet the real Nin. Said that he knew a topless dancer once called Nin. Was I her? No? If my poems could shimmy and writhe, maybe I could, too. I should have hung up right then. Instead I told him the truth: my poems and I are not the same thing. That's why I write them. Poems can say and do and wear whatever they want. Like Dolly Parton in heels and a low-cut blouse as she sashays onto the stage and sings her sexy soul out into the world. You can fantasize all you want, but the truth is, she doesn't give a shit about assholes like you.

Kelly McQuain

DOLLY

At ten even this boy wanted to have them:
what older girls in training bras
had taken to padding, we manufactured
with balloons—swelling our t-shirts
as we sang, my younger sister & I,
to Dolly Parton on the car radio, the slosh
of automated car-wash rollers slapping
against roof & window, & Daddy
for once not yelling at our backseat
performance. I was falling in love
with Dolly, that hillbilly Valkyrie,
her platinum hairdo a spun-sugar miracle,
her hummingbird voice a God-given weapon
against heartache, life's missed takes,
hardscrabble lessons about getting
the things we weren't getting but wanted—
Dolly, the doll I could never have,
her songs hungry & angry & funny—
a golden-throated spiritual connection
to the busty Daisy Mae hidden inside me.
My Dolly-pops squeaked as I rubbed
their knotted nipples, the car wash's
soapy water and brushes almost through,
& Dolly still singing "Here You Come Again"
as Daddy strummed the steering wheel
and lit a cigarette, while Dolly offered
a quick wink, all glitter & glue,
with eyes that could tell if a man
was a happy drunk, a sad or mad one—
& me, a balloon-breasted boy still singing
for a tender bosom to lay his head upon.

Benjamin Anthony Rhodes

IT'S ALL WRONG, BUT IT'S ALRIGHT

It's a cruel joke that the first thing we do
after dying is shit ourselves. If I was
Dolly Parton, I might say something like
That's just God's funny little way of welcoming
us to Heaven—with a roll of Charmin in His hands.
If I was Dolly Parton,
I'd have more rhinestones in my closet
and I wouldn't want to cut off my breasts.

Jenny Molberg

IS IT ALL YOU?

Barbara Walters, in a 1977 interview with Dolly Parton

At twelve I hated them so bad I'd pinch myself at night.
Big Balloons, they called me, Luke laughing

as I somersaulted across the gym floor. In high school
they got me a date to the dance but Casey called me

platinum, my nipples like CDs in a frame.
Big tits, blonde hair. That's who I was. *Lucky.*

Why don't you wear glasses, a distracted teacher once asked,
as if my boobs were too big for my thesis.

I've spent so much time wanting other people
to like me, the Barbie-hard bodies of junior-high girls;

later, philosophy majors with joints. Wanting my body
to change. Changing my body to fit.

After the reduction, my breasts hurt for a year.
I carried little pumps in my pockets where my pink

blood sloshed like liquid change. I've warned men
of my scars, not porn-smooth—my dyed blonde hair

and lifeguard skin, my lines all puckered and pocked.
But do you ever feel that you're a joke? Barbara pushes Dolly.

Her bird laugh tinkles like a bracelet. Barbara
doesn't get it, the work it took to beat the men

to her body's punchline, what is kissed
and is killed. *Anyway I like the kind of person I am,*

Dolly says, which makes me like myself, too.
Over poached eggs wet with buttery sauce

a friend assures me, *one day you'll know*, wink wink,
as she gripes about breastfeeding, as if I'd ever know,

as if all my life I'd been wanting to know,
as if I hadn't made the choice, again and again, not to.

At 87, my grandmother goes in for a radical mastectomy
like my mother ten years before her. She kids:

The women in our family leave more breast tissue
at UT Southwestern than anyone in Dallas!

We're all lighter as we laugh, helping her undress,
her purple scar smiling under what used to be.

Dorianne Laux

DOLLY'S BREASTS

are singing
from the rafters of her chest,
swaying beneath sheeny satin,
suspended in the choreography
of her bra: twin albino dolphins
breaching from her ball gown's
rhinestone cleavage. Her breasts
are sisters praying at twilight, a pair
of fat-cheeked Baptists dreaming
of peaches, her nipples the color
of autumn, two lonely amber eyes.
When she shakes her metallic bodice,
tinsel swimming up her pink fonts
of nourishment, the spotlight hums
and shimmies with them, the audience,
open-mouthed, stunned into silence
as she crosses her legs and bows, her hair
hanging down, a permed curl caught
in that soft, improbable seam.

Marina Carreira

JUST BECAUSE I'M A WOMAN

My wildflower face follows everywhere I go,
there I am, tattoos and piercings preceding
any introduction I make by mouth or tit.
Oh, I'm alarming, arresting the gaze of folks
on the street who don't know what to make
of my drag femininity: my button up a beatitude,
my skirt a pirate flag, eyelashes curled to the gods,
lips pouted to perfection, nails sharpened for all
the glass ceilings. Dolly, they see little old me, figure
I'm just another loon looking for freedom where
the founding fathers promised none for anyone not white
and male. Miss Parton, I pat my own back and smile
in response, rosy cheeks against their chagrin,
feet shuffling though horseshit like a sexy pioneer.

Denise Duhamel

DOLLY PARTON AS SONNET

You're drawn in by her golden hair and bust,
her physical structure, her three octave
soprano sass—glitter and angel dust—
so crafted you're in the Jungian cave

before you know it. Dolly as warrior,
as goddess, as mannequin sprung to life.
Your fairy godmother, the courier
bringing the news it'll turn out all right.

She twists the volta of her childfree hips,
her artifice genuine as a poem
crafted to hold the sublime as it dips
into our collective unconscious, home

to rainbows, banjos, blue eye shadow. Sweet
beat—couplet of her tiny, tapping feet.

Anna Sandy-Elrod

DEAR DOLLY PARTON, I TOO WANTED

to be too much—over-glossed, candy-coated, hair teased to heaven,
heels high, hemline higher, up-to-there, overwhelming the senses
with my existence. I saw your photo on the wall of the Stampede
on my first family trip to Branson and I thought, *there she is.*
Unapologetic. Looming. Blonde and bedazzled. You cracked open
the dirty look, the whisper, the write-off, and dared to be unashamed.
Richest cheap girl ever came from that town. Decide to be beautiful
and you are. Glitter, sequins, a hint of feather. A hint? Never just a hint.
What little girls want is to grow up and get seen. To shine, sparkle, clack.
In Mississippi, I outran the boys, outfought the boys, outclimbed the boys—
up trees and up the ladder. In my head, you, the country girl's best idea
of glamour. And now? You, in my head, nails tap-tapping. I flick
the glitter liner around my eyes for you, Dolly. I lay back and shimmy.
I zip my thigh-high boots up with pliers. I go out and get it, Dolly.

Rosemerry Wahtola Trommer

MAKING BREAKFAST WITH DOLLY

Tonight I read
how Dolly Parton
always wears
high-heeled shoes
in her kitchen.
Don't you?
she asks.
I don't.
I wear old brown
wool slippers.
With orthotics.
I try to imagine myself
strutting into the kitchen
before the kids
go to school,
making smoothies
and scrambled eggs
in my yoga pants,
my long gray sweatshirt,
and my four-inch
Lucite stilettos.
Click, click, click
go the heels
as I teeter toward
the tea cups.
Click, click, click
as I parade
with paper towels
to the place
where the cat
has retched.
Oh, Dolly,
as I slip into
these high-heeled thoughts
I thank you for dressing up the day.

These glammed up ideas
two-step and sashay
through the morning chores,
while meanwhile
my slippered self
marvels at the fun,
but shrugs—
I'm just so darn grateful
for arch support,
for the rubber soles
that ground me
as I sweep up the crumbs,
as I wipe the counters clean.
Grateful that when
the high-heeled thoughts
start to sing—
working 9 to 5—
and *damn*, can they sing,
they invite me
to sing along.

Dion O'Reilly

ODE TO DOLLY

Of course, your breasts—
your Motherland. Your Big Sky.

Your greatness pulling you
forward and forward.

I want to live
in your cleavage.

Gaze at your inch-long nails
as they tick the fretboard.

I will always love you—

your native talent. Your hard
core story and bird-call trill.

Your odd combination
of realness and display.

When I watch you on Jimmy Kimmel,
with your gliss lips and chalk-white,

piled-high perfection,

I feel like Frank O'Hara.
Don't collapse, Dolly Parton.

Don't collapse!
Girl, you're all we've got left.

GUIDE ME AND KEEP ME

Kelli Russell Agodon

DOLLY PARTON IS MY LIFE COACH

Because I worry about everything,
I dream of Dolly making biscuits
and milk gravy while reminding me
my desire is always greater than my fear.

I understand the garden is never tidy
and here you come again with big dreams
and faded jeans. Because the last thing
on my mind were the red shoes

from the bargain store, she tells me
I better get to livin' and there's no such thing
as a dumb blonde, but only silver threads
and golden needles and no one in between

and when she laughs, *My weaknesses*
have always been food and men—
in that order, we order chicken
and dumplins, have a picnic on a cloud

with beauty beyond compare and laugh—
what a way to make a living.

Kerry Trautman

SWEET CRAVINGS

When I write something shitty I hunger for
lines I've lost in my sleep, thirst for

living I've slept through. My poems and I do not
shock and are not easily shocked.

My girlhood Happy Birthday Barbie doll
looked like Dolly Parton—tits and all—

so she sang "Two Doors Down" instead of me.
Falling a little bit in love with every

new poet I meet, I imagine weekend
hotel affairs, minibar bottles scattered on sheets

like an overturned chessboard. My poems
and I wear our seatbelts. When I don't

get a window seat in an airplane, I hunger for
what I can't see myself soaring over.

As a girl I sang Disney from the swing
knowing I'd never seek a stage, barely swayed

at school dances though a *Solid Gold*
dancer in my room. My poems and I don't

wear metallic leather. When I don't
say what I really want to someone,

I hunger for gumption like Doralee in
9 to 5. My bosses never feared tantrums,

boyfriends knew I'd stick around, parents
trusted I'd get home safe and

virginal. My poems and I would always
choose a milkshake over ayahuasca.

We have never smoked, won't lean-in
and whisper an excuse to breathe on

your neck. When I say I never learned to play
chess I mean I can't stop sweet cravings.

ROOSTERS & HENS

Rumors fly fast in southern towns, like the one about my grandfather shacked up with a sixteen-year-old he found hitchhiking to Florida on New Year's Eve. He'd be in jail today, front page news and cancelled, but in 1981 rural Georgia, it's just more grist for the gossip mill. He parades Missy—his *little gal*—at the gas station, five and dime, buys her milkshakes at the Dairy Queen, makes her go in the store to buy his six-packs and cigarettes.

The day he brings her to my house, my mother stands cross-armed and disgusted in the driveway as they argue over his indiscretion. Missy sits in the car snapping her gum and singing along to "Here You Come Again" on the radio. *I've got that 45*, I say shyly, leaning in the window. Her eyes light up, she looks me up and down, reassessing my worth. *Dolly is my idol. I want to be just like her—boobs and all!*

Only four years separate us, but Missy, in her tight jeans, tank top and tall blonde hair, seems much older. Worldly and wise, sure of herself, and when she casually asks me if I've ever kissed a boy, I feel seen for the first time. Missy tells me absolutely nothing, changes the subject when I ask about her family, school, or where she's from.

My grandfather drops us off at the movie theater to see *9 to 5*. Missy slings an arm around my shoulder as we sing along loudly to Dolly's theme song. I can feel the other moviegoers staring, tutting and harrumphing their disapproval. When the scene where Mr. Hart chases Doralee around his desk and she threatens to get the gun out of her purse and shoot his dick off, Missy laughs and claps. *That's just like your granddaddy, but he ain't caught me yet.* Our eyes meet in the dark and even though I'm twelve, her implication is unmistakable. *You'll just have to shoot him then,* I say. *I won't tell.* Her shrieking laugh brings a chorus of *shhhhs* and I taste her bubblegum lipstick for hours after she kisses me unexpectedly on the lips.

Missy is gone by spring. She disappears into the night with an envelope full of Social Security cash and grandpa's gun, doesn't leave a note. He rages for days, duped and lonely, begs Mom for money to buy his Pabst tall boys.

I don't tell them that Missy made one last stop before she left town. The morning after her disappearance, I find a small brown bag propped on the windowsill of my room. Inside is the 45 of "9 to 5" with big-haired, busty Dolly on the sleeve marching off to work carrying a paint roller like a staff, a garden hoe, blueprints, jumper cables, work boots, and other odd job tools slung over her back. I've lost track of how many times I've watched *9 to 5*, spoken Dolly's dialogue back to the TV, and wondered if Missy ever had to use my grandfather's gun, or turned any roosters into hens to get where she was going.

Denise Duhamel & Julie Marie Wade

DOLLY PARTON GHAZAL

When I was a kid, I thought they made *Hello, Dolly*
about you! You dreamt the Hollywood sign read *Dolly-*

wood, and one day it did in East Tennessee! *Dolly
Parton's Imagination Library*, a $35 custom license plate Dolly

fans in the Volunteer State can purchase as of 2016. Dolly,
an avid reader, you gift books to TN children. Dolly

you knew how books keep on giving, unlike Slinkys and dollies.
Each move I'd box my poetry volumes and roll them on a dolly

up the U-Haul ramp. The best books last forever, as you must, Dolly—
bringing together cowboys and drag queens dressed as Dolly,

Appalachian Pride and LGBTQ pride side by side. Dolly,
how many have chosen you as a write-in candidate? *Dolly*

Parton for President! Jane Fonda as your running mate? Oh, Dolly,
how you sparkle, star-spangled, and wise as the Dalai

Lama. You have been my spiritual leader, Dolly.
I prayed to your tiny waist as I gobbled Hostess and Dolly

Madison cakes, to your big wigs as my hair thinned, Dolly.
Your authenticity fluttered fake eyelashes, Dolly,

and I wanted to see the world as you saw it. Dolly,
I feel the room swaying. Promise you'll never go away, Dolly.

Roberta Schultz

INTERVIEW

No high school wanted to pay
a newly-minted M.A.
(with no experience)
to teach English
and coach volleyball.

But, I decided if I wore my silky new
powder blue pantsuit inspired
by *The Porter Wagoner Show*,
someone, somewhere would see
my shine.

So, I drove my '65 VW Beetle
out Route 32 to Clermont County.
Told that principal of course
I could coach volleyball—
even though I'd last
played in 7th grade—
went on and on about
how I loved to write,
sprayed sass
around his office
like Aqua Net.

I could tell I would not get the gig.

Halfway home, the tie rod scraped
the paint of the *do not pass* line.
I imagined Dolly driving back roads
home from a long country tour.

A sleek and can-do woman jumped out
of my car, hoisted thin rusty metal
from the road, lashed it to the axle
with her matching beaded hair tie.

I brushed dirt from my sparkly
sky blue ass, waved and blew kisses
at the farm boys whistling past
in their Ford pickup truck.

Makayla Gay

CONVERSATIONS WITH DOLLY PARTON AT 3 A.M.

Sweetheart,
      she says, her voice like the
      opening strum on an autoharp,
Once you let anyone steal your sunshine
you are your own rainy day.
      She holds my head like Madonna
      and kisses my bangs.
      She reminds me how she birthed entire
      patch-worked mountains from her hips.
      She's Gaia,
            spangled in rhinestones, hairspray
            and long, almond nails.
      She gets called trash
      but trills like you wouldn't believe.
      Our holy mother,
            of looking like a trick and
            letting all sorts of sinners seek
            shelter somewhere.
You got mountains inside you,
sticks and rock and ramble.
She holds my face and laughs like honey on biscuits.
It's hard enough being a woman,
especially if you like making a show of it.
      She adjusts the cups of her brassiere
               and tectonics crash.
Sometimes,
you gotta let things go simply because they are heavy.
      She smudges the coal dust around her eyes
        and two coats of mascara.
          A swallow won't sing
            unless prompted.
If you can't stand to give all your love to one—
        she says, knowing full well
      what it means to have all your love
          fracked away.

Micah Ruelle

VISITATION

For Momma

I dreamed one night
I was falling like a star
through the neon lights
of Vegas. Sound burst
forth through lights:
first piano
then guitar
then banjo—
"The Seeker" played
loud and clear as day.
Dolly's neon cowgirl
silhouette loomed over me
as she climbed the cosmic stage.
Applause rumbled through
the ether though the only ones there
were my momma and me,
crying into a Texas-sized
mug of beer. I was holding
my momma who cried at the words,
You are a keeper. Dolly,
our celestial mother,
our own Mother Mary,
she cradled us in the ether to
soothe the mother-wound in us both.
The part that splintered some
point now lost in memory.
I saw my mother's deep tear,
and she saw mine, all the while
Dolly sang the notes that would sew
up both: *won't you show me the way?*

Chin-Sun Lee

RESCUE

We were at a Walmart Auto Center somewhere in Alabama, which wasn't on my bucket list, but better than being dead in a ditch. They said it would be another hour, so I told M, *Might as well forage for food.* I'm like a dog that way—my stomach never forgets mealtime. We went into the store and paid for sad cold sandwiches at the self-checkout. Those machines always make me feel like the end times are near. D called, but I was still pissed at him and let it ring. Up until then, it was all serendipity: M's last-minute invite to St. George Island, my co-worker wanting extra shifts, us finding a honky-tonk seafood shack still open after the long drive that first night. "Islands in the Stream" came on—the Dolly/Kenny version—and we got up from our stools to twirl around and shimmy with our beers in hand. I said, *Someone told me listening to her saved his life.* M said, *Wish I had a good rescue story.* The next morning, beyond our balcony, clear blue waves and white sand. We found a beach umbrella in the trash that was janky, like M's car, but useable. Steps away from our rental was a seafood joint with an outdoor bar. We ate fried shrimp in plastic baskets lined with checkered paper, drank Cuba Libres, and bitched about how our men were failing us. I often see exit signs too late or when it's not convenient. I left my sunglasses on the ledge outside our room one night and they were still there the next day. Another night, I left my wet swimsuit at the restaurant and only remembered after they closed. While M was sleeping, I went back. The lights in the kitchen were on, the door was unlocked, and there on the counter was my bag with the swimsuit! Our luck ran out on the way back. Or maybe it didn't. I was driving, going 80 mph on I-10, when the road started feeling bumpy. I slowed down, but the bumps and rattling got worse. I said, *I'm pulling over.* Just as I came to a full stop, a rubber tube flew off and rolled into the ditch on the passenger side. We got out and stared at the naked tire. A truck whizzed past with an ad for Dollywood. M yelled, *Hello Dolly*! and we said how funny it was she popped up at the start and end of our trip. After M called AAA, she said, *I can't believe we're not dead.*

Karen Head

INSTRUCTIONS FOR MY BURIAL CLOTHES

Sometimes I dream
Dolly Parton is my aunt.
I'm about twelve.
She comes to visit
at Easter,
brings me chocolates,
jelly beans,
and makeup.

My mother frowns,
hurries around the kitchen
with other female relatives—
they are all wearing sackcloth.
Dolly sits beside me,
plays a guitar and sings,
her long red-glittered nails
click against the frets.

When I say,
Do not bury me in a suit,
I want to go out in sequins,
my mother shakes her head,
wonders where I learned such excess.

Lynn Melnick

WILL HE BE WAITING FOR ME

For Stella

sings my daughter on a stifling spring night
when she's come out of the a/c to retrieve something
or other and I say, *oh wow, that's a deep cut* and she groans

because she's a teenager now and she groans at a lot of things
I like, and that's okay. All lockdown we shared a room
while we worked, and we listened to Dolly, the big hits

and the lesser hits, the covers, the songs that sound
like others of her songs. I gave her the trivia as I found it,
like how Dolly wrote "Two Doors Down"

when she was sad not to eat fried clams at Howard Johnson's
because she was at one point always on a diet but then she went
anyway, to the party of fried seafood

and I want more of that abandon, more love, more odes
to everyday pleasure. All lockdown we ate snacks
while we worked, snacks from packages meant for a commute,

and I kept thinking how my daughter is on the precipice
of leaving me because that is what she is supposed to do.
One day she asked, *So, do you think he'll be waiting for her?*

and I looked up from my laptop at my radiant girl
and answered, *You know, I never thought about that before*
as Dolly sang, *he will be, won't he?*

Julie Marie Wade

IN THE DREAM, DOLLY OFFERS TO OFFICIATE

For Angie

Mid-autumn. Smoky Mountains. Here in the land she and my love are from. Here on the day we thought would never come. Yellow birch. Black cherry. Northern red oak. Our rainbow. And long ago, before the blight, American chestnut everywhere. I dream them back in. I dream us beneath them. Once, this land was only a postcard to me. Bonnie flew to Dollywood from the West Coast and wrote *Guess where I am!* Exclamation mark, not question mark, because we already knew. On my placemat, the state was copper, like a penny, and longer than you'd think it would be. Until I drove it, Memphis to Knoxville, Memphis to Chattanooga, the droll hours with my love beside me. Listening to Dolly, of course: "Islands in the Stream," "Jolene," "I Will Always Love You." That one twice, three times: Dolly, Whitney, then Dolly again. We have lived through the blight, the long ban. Now we stand in the shadow of the bright trees as a spangled woman walks toward us, humming. The leaves in her hair, golden and cordate. Her hands extended, the sparkling nails. *Guess what we're here to celebrate!* Exclamation mark, not question mark, because we already knew.

Robert Gwaltney

BUTTERFLIES

Take us to that trampoline sky,
hide us under a thunder cloud,

to a thing no one else should see,
before it pulls us right back down.

Glory the jump, rusted metronome
of springs, an angel calling from above.

Fly, fly, butterfly.
Boys like us have secret wings.

Sun don't care—keeps spilling down,
gleaming naked through your hair.

Dolly's voice comes through
the screen, streaming

from your sister's window, a scratched LP,
all of this a *rare and gentle thing*.

Do you remember back to ten,
when you loved me in the sky?

I jump high and you keep low.
You made me promise not to tell.

David-Matthew Barnes

WALKING TO KMART TO BUY A DOLLY PARTON ALBUM

Someone protects me when I'm ten: a boy
in my class. He's stronger than the others.
He waits for me each day, walks me home.
He's convinced I'll be the next

Nancy Drew and encourages me to open up
my own detective agency. He colors the green
construction paper signs we tape in store windows.
We wait for our first clients and when no one

calls, he tells me, *Don't worry. Business will
pick up.* When I walk down the road we live on
to go to Kmart to buy a Dolly Parton album,
I imagine what it will be like to marry him,

the defender of my honor. He makes me think
of Disney princes, love songs belted out
by animated women, glass slippers. I break
open wide when he kisses my cheek, the spot

right below the bruise. When I crawl out of
windows at night, to call the police
when my mother and her lover are beaten
up in love again, he's there to turn

the record player on. He makes me listen
until we know every word Dolly sings by heart.
While I wait until the coast is clear and it's safe
to go home again, he offers me his version of

"But You Know I Love You" and when he finishes,
he's surprised to see me cry. On instinct,
he holds me until the music ends. I pretend
we live together, in a home of our own. We duet

each night after dinner. We line dance, arm in arm.
We learn to play the fiddle and the banjo. In spring,
Aunt Dolly comes to visit, writes a love song
for the two of us to always keep. A week

before my mother makes us move again, the other
boys try to run me down, chase me with bikes and bats,
but he hits them hard with closed fists, as if he's holding
my heart in both hands. As if he will
never let me go.

ONE YEAR BEFORE HIS DEATH, PETER HUJAR SEES DOLLY PARTON

Very depressing news, Fran said
after Peter's dismal doctor's report.
They shuffled slowly down East 61st Street,
Peter hollow-cheeked, front teeth protruding,
and unshaven like so many men back then.
Although his appetite was long-gone,
he stared longingly into Madame Romaine de Lyon,
remembering the taste of their $30 omelettes,
a small fortune at the time.
Fran said, *my treat.*

At the table, hunched over menus,
they were grief-stricken at the news,
but then there was a buzz, a change
in the temperature of the room.
Dolly Parton walked in, blonde hair
teased and sprayed, red lips
over breasts like a shelf. A star.
Peter came to life at the sight of her,
his eyes sparkled like the flashbulbs
he used to capture so many
celebrities with his camera.
She walked past the table
of a soon-to-be dead man,
left him feeling high for weeks after.

Years after his death, Fran Lebowitz
recounted the story to her friend Dolly Parton,
who asked: *Why didn't you stop me?*
I would have been happy to talk with him.
Fran said: *But I didn't know you then.*
And in that very Dolly way, she replied:
I would have still talked to you two.

Emma Bolden

ASEXUAL ODE TO DOLLY PARTON

That summer I listened to "Jolene" six
times every time I got in the car & I sang
along hard enough to believe it, that it

was as simple as there always being an other
waiting, flame-haired, spring-breathed, to take
whatever man whenever I wanted to mine him.

As if the problem wasn't my longing. Lack thereof.
& there was so much longing locked into
Dolly's looping curls. I thought if I loud-sang

enough, hard-listened enough, I could learn it.
How to woman myself the way everyone wanted
me to. O Dolly, patron saint of shoulder fringe

& sequins, high priestess of Lee Press Ons
& hairspray, how long your longing held me,
summer-voiced, soft enough to show me

how every kind of love's a force that sends you
to your knees, begging, even if I couldn't love—
again—in a way I could make any other understand.

teri elam

A DOLLY PARTON KINDA LOVE

In this green & yellow kitchen lived this family's soul.
Home. Fish-fried Fridays, Mrs. Butterworth-Saturdays,
Between. Its chants: *O Mighty Isis! & Soulll Trainnn!*
Beans snapped, collards rolled & chopped, simmering,
Its sweet peppery pot likker, their moonshine. Near night-
Fall when the sisters' nappy, unfettered hair would be
Reimagined for church the next day. Kitchen, now smoking,
Hot comb on the stove, radio blasting the Ohio Players
Rollercoaster of love, Say what?! This before you grew
Up, met *the one* that got her way, then got away. Your
Soul trying to not become the Jonah to her whale. When
All you needed was that Dolly Parton kinda love she'd
Warble thru the tiny TV in that kitchen—on her pushup-
Pink parasol'd walk to a swing hanging from a cloud rapping
I hope life treats you kind & I hope you have all you
Dreamed of, her voice, peppermint-stick goodness to your
Elementary school ears, eyes, & heart. Back when you first
Felt butterflies flutter, a feeling you didn't know what was
Then, but you've chased with a net ever since.

ACKNOWLEDGMENTS

Though there are not words adequate enough to express gratitude to Dolly Parton and her team, editors Dustin and Julie say, *Thank you for letting your light shine down on* Let Me Say This: A Dolly Parton Poetry Anthology. *Thank you for allowing us to use the gorgeous Fran Strine photo as the anthology cover. And thank you Jeff Kleinman, Kyle McClain, and Peter Laird for making the dream come to be.*

Julie and Dustin offer thanks to the muralists and photographers who made the back cover possible. Thank you for amplifying Dolly in public spaces and reminding the world of her continued light and persistent presence.

Julie and Dustin also extend a kaleidoscope of butterflies to Kim and the Madville team: *Thank you for flying with us in enthusiasm and sheer joy during the journey, and for believing in us every step of the way.*

The editors also share their gratitude for the following generous supporters who ensured there were no financial barriers to the submission process: Gareth Bloemeke, Jaye Bloemeke, Julie E. Bloemeke, Mark Bloemeke, Dustin Brookshire, Kelly Cockerham, John Cowley, Chris Dielmann, Chad Frame, Harbor Editions, Danielle Lemay, Limp Wrist Press on behalf of the Wild & Precious Life Series and *Limp Wrist*, Jim and Marilyn O'Neill, Elisia and Rob Payne, Gaye and Tom Payne, Rick Sanchez, Mel Sherrer, Rob Warrington, Matthew Dean Wilder, and an anonymous benefactor.

The editors are appreciative of the information documented in the following publications and online resources that were used for their Dollyverse research for this anthology: Dolly Parton, *Dolly: My Life and Other Unfinished Business*, New York: Harper Collins, 1994, and Dolly Parton, with Robert K. Oermann, *Dolly Parton: Songteller, My Life in Lyrics*, Chronicle Books: San Francisco, 2020; Duane Gordon's *Dollymania* (www.dollymania.net); *Dolly Parton Online* (dollyon-line. com); Dolly's official website (dollyparton.com); Dolly's official Instagram account (@dollyparton); Library of Congress; NPR; *Dolly Parton's America*, hosted by Jad Abumrad and Shima Oliaee.

Dustin extends his love and appreciation to his partner, Chris, for his patience and unwavering support. He offers Chris a cup of gratitude for the hours upon hours of being a concert of one while Dustin sings along with Dolly. Dustin's love and appreciation to Chris could fill every inch of Dollywood three times over. Dustin thanks the following friends for their counsel and encouragement during his work on this project: Emma Bolden, John Cowley, Chris Dielmann, Denise Duhamel, Beth Gylys, Lynn Melnick, Gregg Shapiro, and Reid Strauss. A hearty thank you is extended to Travis Collinsworth for his quick assistance. And to the person he'll always go two doors down with to laugh and drink and have a party, Julie E. Bloemeke, he says this: *Thank you for partnering with me on this journey through the Dollyverse. An anthology, even one that is a true love and passion of the soul, is a lot of work—I couldn't have done this without you. I'll always love you.*

Julie shares big Dolly love and gratitude to her family—Mark, Gareth, and Jaye Bloemeke—for offering support and enduring her out-of-tune Dolly crooning. She also thanks the following big-hearted folks who embody true *show me the way* love in their listening and insight: Kelly Cockerham, River Grey, Robert Gwaltney, Collin Kelley, Ben Kline, Sarah Taylor Myers, and Matthew Dean Wilder. Heaps of love and thanks to the Virginia Center for the Creative Arts and the extended #JToledo5 crew: Kari Ann Ebert, Ken Hart, Chin-Sun Lee, Brian O'Hare, Eric Sasson, L.J. Sysko, and Kerry Trautman. Bird Lake love and gratitude to Brent and Lisa Trent for cottage space to write and work, and special thanks to Becca Raymond, Ellen Compton, and Catherine Cowan Compton for being the embodiment of *everybody's neighbor.*

And every last glittering diamond for Dustin Brookshire who shines the world into a better place just by being. Let me say this: *Thank you for inviting me to create this Dolly book with you, with all the love and butterflies. From the moment we serendipitously spied Dolly's photo above us in Tennessee, she has guided us. You make the work a party, and I will always love you too.*

CREDITS & NOTES

All song writers listed in parenthesis at first song mention, thereafter only song title is cited.

Kelli Russell Agodon's "Dolly Parton is My Life Coach" references song titles and lyrics from the following songs: "Big Dreams and Faded Jeans," "Better Get to Livin'," "Jolene," "9 to 5," and "The Bargain Store," (all written by Dolly Parton). It also references the following songs performed by Parton but written by other artists: "Here You Come Again" (Barry Mann and Cynthia Weil); "Dumb Blonde" (Curly Putman); "The Last Thing On My Mind" (Tom Paxton); "Silver Threads and Golden Needles" (Dick Reynolds and Jack Rhodes); "Islands in the Stream" (Barry, Maurice, and Robin Gibb); and "Red Shoes" (Parton and Linda Perry). *My weaknesses have always been food and men—in that order,* is a direct quote from Parton.

Kelli Russell Agodon's "Were it not for the moonlight" draws on references from the album *Slow Dancing With the Moon* by Parton. Truvy's Cuppa Cuppa Cuppa Cake is a reference from the film, *Steel Magnolias*. *Grace and Frankie* is the TV show where Parton plays God in a cameo. The poem also references "Jolene" and "Here You Come Again." The last stanzas reference the lip sync between The Vivienne and Yvie Oddly to "Why'd You Come in Here Lookin' Like That" (Randy Thomas and Bob Carlisle) on *RuPaul's Drag Race All Stars* season 7, episode 6.

Nin Andrews's "How do you, as a woman, dare to write about sex?" was published in *Limp Wrist*.

David-Matthew Barnes's "Walking to Kmart to Buy a Dolly Parton Album" was published in *The Southeast Review* and *Recasting Masculinity*. The poem references the song title "But You Know I Love You" (Mike Settle).

Nicky Beer's "Drag Day at Dollywood" was published in her collection *Real Phonies and Genuine Fakes* (Milkweed Editions, 2022).

Julie E. Bloemeke's "Dolly Would" incorporates interview quotes directly from Parton in the trailer and episode 9 of *Dolly Parton's America*, as well as Bloemeke's personal notes from the *Better Day* tour, August 3, 2011, and the *Pure & Simple* tour, November 18, 2016.

Emma Bolden's "Asexual Ode to Dolly Parton" was published in *Limp Wrist*. The poem references the song title "Jolene."

Dustin Brookshire's "Dolly at the Fox Theater (2008)" was published in *Harbor Review*.

Phillip Watts Brown's "If You Play 'Jolene' at 33 rpm" was published in *Limp Wrist*. The poem incorporates lyrics from the song "Jolene."

Marina Carreira's "Just Because I'm a Woman" is also the title of a song by Parton.

Denise Duhamel, **Maureen Seaton**, and **Julie Marie Wade**'s "Seventy-Five Lines for Dolly's Seventy-Fifth" references "Cologne" (Parton); "The Gambler" (Don Schlitz);

"Islands in the Stream"; "I Will Always Love You" (Parton); "Rainbowland" (Miley Cyrus and Parton); and "Two Sides to Every Story" (Bill Owens and Parton).

Denise Duhamel and **Julie Marie Wade**'s "Dolly Parton Ghazal" was published in *Limp Wrist*. The poem references the play title *Hello, Dolly!* and incorporates lyrics from the song of the same name–written by Jerry Herman–and from the song "Where Beauty Lives in Memory" (Parton).

teri elam's "A Dolly Parton Kinda Love" incorporates lyrics from "Love Rollercoaster" (Billy Beck, Leroy Bonner, Sugarfoot, Clarence "Satch" Satchell, Marshall "Rock" Jones, Marvin Pierce, Ralph Middlebrooks, James "Diamond" Williams and performed by The Ohio Players). Additionally, the poem incorporates lyrics from "I Will Always Love You" (Parton).

Rupert Fike's "The Porter Wagoner Show" was published in *Limp Wrist*.

Diamond Forde's "The Great Equalizer" incorporates lyrics from "Jolene."

Chad Frame's "The Intimate Biography" incorporates an abridged title of Alana Nash's *Dolly: The Intimate Biography of Dolly Parton* (Panther, 1979) and lyrics from the song "Coat of Many Colors" (Parton).

Makayla Gay's "Conversations with Dolly Parton at 3 a.m.," in another version, was published in *Still: The Journal*.

Tyler Gillespie's "Dolly Parton argues a theory of linguistics. posits" incorporates lyrics from the song "Dumb Blonde."

Kari Gunter-Seymour's "Perfect Pitch" was published in her collection *A Place So Deep Inside America It Can't Be Seen* (Sheila-Na-Gig Editions, 2020). The poem incorporates the song title and lyrics from "Jolene" as well as the song title "9 to 5."

Robert Gwaltney's "Butterflies" incorporates lyrics from "Love is Like a Butterfly," (Parton).

Karen Head's "Instructions for My Burial Clothes" was published in her collection *Sassing* (WordTech Editions, 2009) and *Limp Wrist*.

Raye Hendrix's "Eugene, Oregon/Homesick" references the song title "Eugene, Oregon" (Parton).

Collin Kelley's "Roosters & Hens" was published in *Limp Wrist*. The poem incorporates the song title "Here You Come Again" and the movie title *9 to 5*.

Dorianne Laux's "Dolly's Breasts" was published in *The American Poetry Review, Limp Wrist*, and Laux's *The Book of Women* (Red Dragonfly Press, 2012).

Dorianne Laux's "Dolly Said 'No' to Elvis" was published in *Limp Wrist* under a different title. The poem mentions the movie title *The Bodyguard*. It also incorporates the phrase *a mighty thing* which is a direct quote from Parton.

Chin-Sun Lee's "R E S C U E" references the song title "Here You Come Again."

Arden Levine's "If this song seems strange, it's just because I don't know how to pray." takes its title from the song "Travelin' Prayer," written and originally recorded by Billy Joel and later covered by Parton. Additionally, the poem incorporates lyrics from both the original and covered versions of "Travelin' Prayer." The epigraph comes from a statement made by Parton as documented in *MTV News* when her album *The Grass Is Blue* was released (1999).

Kelly McQuain's "Dolly," under another title, was published in *Limp Wrist*. The poem incorporates the song title "Here You Come Again."

Katie Manning's "Dolly, When I Met You There Was Peace" was published in *Limp Wrist*. The poem incorporates the movie titles *Rhinestone Cowboy* and *Mary Poppins*.

Lynn Melnick's "Will He Be Waiting for Me" is also the title of a song written by Parton and incorporates lyrics from it. The poem also mentions the song "Two Doors Down" (Parton).

Jenny Molberg's "IS IT ALL YOU?" incorporates quotes from a December 6, 1977, Barbara Walters interview with Parton.

Rachel Morgan's "These Mountains" incorporates the song title "My Tennessee Mountain Home" (Parton).

Caridad Moro-Gronlier's "Never Did Say So" was published in *Limp Wrist*. The poem includes an epigraph that incorporates the song title "To Daddy" (Parton).

Carolyn Oliver's "I overhear a boy humming 'Jolene' while he practices long division" was published in *Limp Wrist*. The poem incorporates the song title "Jolene."

Jeffrey Perkins's "Nashville" was published in *Limp Wrist* and incorporates lyrics from "You're the Only One" (Carole Bayer Sager and Bruce Roberts). "San Fernando" incorporates lyrics from "Here You Come Again."

Stephen Roger Powers's "Cleoparton" was inspired by Dolly's participation in the 2004 Dollywood Festival of Nations Parade. This poem was published in *The Broad River Review*, *Limp Wrist*, and Powers's collection *The Follower's Tale* (Salmon Poetry, 2009).

Steven Reigns's "One Year Before His Death, Peter Hujar Sees Dolly Parton" is based on a sighting story told during *An Evening with Fran Lebowitz* at the Morgan Library with Joel Smith in 2018. Peter Hujar (1934–1987) was an American photographer best known for his black and white portraits. Hujar photographed and befriended many celebrities, and he succumbed to AIDS at the age of 53.

Linda Neal Reising's "Dolly's Debut" references both the song title "Dumb Blonde" and Dolly's first appearance on *The Porter Wagoner Show* on September 5, 1967.

Benjamin Anthony Rhodes's "It's All Wrong, But It's Alright" was published in *Freezeray Poetry*. The poem's title is also the title of a song written by Parton.

Micah Ruelle's "Visitation" incorporates the song title and lyrics from "The Seeker" (Parton).

Anna Sandy-Elrod's "Dear Dolly Parton, I Too Wanted" was published in *Limp Wrist*.

L.J. Sysko's "The Yassification of Dolly Parton" references the song title "Jolene."

Kerry Trautman's "Sweet Cravings" incorporates the song titles "Two Doors Down" and "9 to 5."

Rosemerry Wahtola Trommer's "Making Breakfast with Dolly" was published in *Limp Wrist*. The poem incorporates lyrics from the song "9 to 5."

Dan Vera's "Pilgrimage" incorporates the following titles of songs: "Jolene," "Islands in the Stream," and "A Smoky Mountain Christmas" (Parton).

Isaiah Vianese's "My Broadway Crush Covers 'Wildflowers'" incorporates the title of a song of the same name written by Parton.

Donna Vorreyer's "Dolly Refuses the Nomination" is inspired by Parton's initial refusal of a nomination to the Rock and Roll Hall of Fame. On March 14, 2022, Parton shared in an Instagram post that she felt she had not earned that right. On April 29, 2022, in an interview with NPR's *Morning Edition*, Parton expressed a change of heart and stated she would accept if voted in. Parton was inducted in the Rock and Roll Hall of Fame on November 5, 2022.

Julie Marie Wade's "In the Dream, Dolly Offers to Officiate" references the following song titles: "Islands in the Stream," "Jolene," and "I Will Always Love You."

CONTRIBUTOR BIOS

Nin Andrews's (she/her) most recent collection of poetry, *The Last Orgasm*, was published by Etruscan Press in 2020. Find Nin online at ninandrews.com.

Kelli Russell Agodon's (she/her) newest book is *Dialogues with Rising Tides* (Copper Canyon Press) and was a finalist for the Washington State Book Awards. She is the co-founder of Two Sylvias Press where she works as an editor and book cover designer, and she also teaches at Pacific Lutheran University's low-res MFA program, the Rainier Writing Workshop. Find her online at agodon.com or twosylviaspress.com.

Author of the novel *Like Light, Like Music* (West Virginia University Press, 2020), **Lana K. W. Austin**'s (she/her) writing has been in *Mid-American Review, Columbia Journal, Sou'wester*, etc. Winner of the 2019 Alabama State Poetry Society Book of the Year Award, the 2019 Hackney Poetry Award, the 2018 Words & Music Poetry Award & *Still: The Journal*'s Judge's Choice Story Award, Austin has been a finalist and semi-finalist in many other competitions. Her MFA is from GMU. Austin's poetry collection, *Blood Harmony*, is from Iris Press. Austin teaches creative writing at the University of Alabama in Huntsville and is in the Peauxdunque Writers Alliance.

David-Matthew Barnes (he/him) is the bestselling author of sixteen novels, three collections of poetry, seven short stories, and more than seventy stage plays that have been performed in three languages in twelve countries. His literary work has appeared in over one hundred publications. An avid movie reviewer, he is the host of the film review web series *Filtinsel*. He lives in Sacramento, California.

Nicky Beer (she/her) is a bi/queer writer, and the author of *Real Phonies and Genuine Fakes* (Milkweed, 2022). Her first two books, *The Diminishing House* (Carnegie Mellon, 2010) and *The Octopus Game* (Carnegie Mellon, 2015), were both winners of the Colorado Book Award for Poetry. She has received honors from the National Endowment for the Arts, MacDowell, the Poetry Foundation, and the Bread Loaf Writers' Conference. She is an associate professor at the University of Colorado Denver, where she is a poetry editor for *Copper Nickel*.

Emma Bolden (she/her) is the author of *House Is an Enigma* (Southeast Missouri State University Press), *medi(t)ations* (Noctuary Press), and *Maleficae* (GenPop Books). The recipient of a Creative Writing Fellowship from the NEA, her work has appeared in *The Norton Introduction to Literature, The Best American Poetry, The Best Small Fictions*, and such journals as the *Mississippi Review, The Seneca Review, StoryQuarterly, Prairie Schooner, TriQuarterly,* and *Shenandoah*. She currently serves as Associate Editor-in-Chief for *Tupelo Quarterly* and an Editor of *Screen Door Review*. Her memoir, *The Tiger and the Cage*, is forthcoming from Soft Skull Press in 2022.

Phillip Watts Brown (he/him) received his MFA in poetry from Oregon State University. His work has appeared or is forthcoming in several journals, including *Ninth Letter, The Common, Ruminate, Spillway, Limp Wrist,* and *Tahoma Literary Review.* He and his husband live in northern Utah, where he works as a graphic designer. He also serves as a poetry editor for the journal *Halfway Down the Stairs.*

Marina Carreira (she/they) is a queer Luso-American poet artist from Newark, NJ. She is the author of *Tanto Tanto* (Cavankerry Press, 2022) and *Save the Bathwater* (Get Fresh Books, 2018). She has exhibited her art at Morris Museum, ArtFront Galleries, West Orange Arts Council, Monmouth University Center for the Arts, among others. She holds an MFA in Creative Writing and is pursuing a D.Litt. in Fine Arts and Media. Keep up with her at hellomarinacarreira.com.

Denise Duhamel's (she/her) most recent books of poetry are *Second Story* (Pittsburgh, 2021) and *Scald* (2017). *Blowout* (2013) was a finalist for the National Book Critics Circle Award. A recipient of fellowships from the Guggenheim Foundation and the National Endowment for the Arts, she is a distinguished university professor in the MFA program at Florida International University in Miami.

teri elam (she/her) is a multi-genre storyteller. Her poems and essays have been published, in print and online, in journals like *Prairie Schooner, Limp Wrist, december magazine, Heavy Feather Review, Birmingham Poetry Review,* and most recently, *The Future of Black: Afrofuturism and Black Comics Poetry.* She's a film reviewer for *Incluvie* and a Stowe Sidewalk Narrative Lab Alum for her screenplay #WifeLessons. Her screenplay, *BattleGround,* is a 2022 quarterfinalist for the ScreenCraft Feature Competition.

Rupert Fike's (he/him) second collection of poems, *Hello the House,* was named a Book All Georgians Should Read in 2018 by The Georgia Center for the Book. It also won the Haas Poetry Prize from Snake Nation Press. He was named a Finalist as Georgia Author of the Year after the publication of his first collection, *Lotus Buffet* (Brick Road Poetry Press, 2011). His stories and poems have appeared in *The Southern Poetry Review, The Sun, Scalawag Magazine, The Georgetown Review, A&U: America's AIDS Magazine, The Flannery O'Connor Review, The Buddhist Poetry Review, Kestrel, Natural Bridge,* and others.

Diamond Forde (she/her) is the author of *Mother Body* (Saturnalia Books). Her work has appeared in *ANMLY, Ninth Letter, Massachusetts Review* and more. Find her online at diamondforde.com.

Chad Frame (he/him) is the author of *Little Black Book* (Finishing Line Press, 2022) and two forthcoming chapbooks, *Cryptid* and *Smoking Shelter.* He is Director of the Montgomery County Poet Laureate Program and a Poet Laureate Emeritus of Montgomery County, PA, the Poetry Editor of *Ovunque Siamo,* a founding member of the No River Twice poetry/improv performance troupe, and Founder of the Caesura Poetry Festival and Retreat. His work has appeared in *Rattle, Pedestal, Barrelhouse, Rust+Moth,* and elsewhere, including on iTunes from the Library of Congress, and was sent to the moon as part of the Lunar Codex Project.

Makayla Gay (she/her) hails from Southeastern Kentucky. Her family spent their summers in Gatlinburg, Tennessee where 100-foot neon Dolly's blinded every hotel room. She attended Converse College in South Carolina where she learned to smoke and curse. She is a MFA candidate in Poetry at Sarah Lawrence. She lives in Brooklyn.

Tyler Gillespie (he/him) is the author of the nonfiction book *The Thing about Florida: Exploring a Misunderstood State* (UPF, 2021) and two poetry collections *Florida Man: Poems* (Red Flag Poetry, 2018) and *the nature machine!* (Autofocus Books, forthcoming, spring 2023). He teaches writing at Ringling College of Art + Design in Sarasota, FL.

Kari Gunter-Seymour (she/her) is a ninth generation Appalachian, Poet Laureate of Ohio and an Academy of American Poets Laureate Fellow. Her poetry collections include *Alone in the House of My Heart* (Ohio University Swallow Press, 2022) and *A Place So Deep Inside America It Can't Be Seen* (Sheila Na Gig Editions, 2020), winner of the 2020 Ohio Poet of the Year Award. Her work has been featured on *Verse Daily, World Literature Today, the New York Times* and *Poem-a-Day*.

Robert Gwaltney (he/him), an award-winning author of southern fiction, resides in Georgia. His debut novel, *The Cicada Tree*, is the 2022 winner of the Somerset Award for Literary Fiction. An active member of the Atlanta literary community, he also serves as a board member for Broadleaf Writers Association. By day, he is the Vice President of Easter Seals North Georgia, Inc., Children Services, a non-profit supporting children with disabilities and other special needs. His work has appeared in such publications as *The Signal Mountain Review, The Blue Mountain Review,* and *The Dead Mule School of Southern Literature.* "Butterflies" is his first published poem.

Beth Gylys (she/her) is a Distinguished Professor at Georgia State University in its Department of English and an award-winning poet whose fifth book of poems (a collaboration with the poets Cathy Carlisi and Jennifer Wheelock), *The Conversation Turns to Wide-Mouth Jars*, was published in August 2022. Her fourth collection of poetry, *Body Braille* (Iris Books 2020), was named a Book All Georgians Should Read in 2021. Her work has appeared in many journals and anthologies—most recently on the *Best American Poetry* blog and in *West Branch*—and her chapbook, *After My Father*, is forthcoming.

Karen Head (she/her) is the author of six books of poetry, including *Lost on Purpose, My Paris Year*, and *Sassing*. She is the Poet Laureate of Fulton County (GA), the Poet Laureate of Waffle House, the editor of *Atlanta Review*, and a professor at the Missouri University of Science & Technology, where she is the Director of the Center for Arts & Technology. She used to spend a lot of time in Nashville, and had the privilege of meeting Dolly Parton one fine fall day. It is an experience she will treasure until she takes her last breath.

Raye Hendrix (she/they) is a writer from Alabama. She is the author of two poetry chapbooks, *Every Journal is a Plague Journal* (Bottlecap Press) and *Fire Sermons* (Ghost City Press), and is the poetry editor at Press Pause Press. The winner of the Keene Prize for Literature and *Southern Indiana Review*'s Patricia Aakhus Award, their work appears in or is forthcoming from *American Poetry Review, Poet Lore, Adroit Journal, Poetry*

Northwest, *32 Poems*, and others. Raye holds two degrees from Auburn University, an MFA from the University of Texas at Austin, and is a PhD candidate at the University of Oregon.

Collin Kelley (he/him) is a poet, novelist, and journalist from Atlanta, GA. His latest poetry collection is *Wonder & Wreckage: New & Selected Poems, 2003-2023* from Poetry Atlanta Press.

Dorianne Laux's (she/her) sixth collection, *Only As the Day is Long: New and Selected Poems* was named a finalist for the 2020 Pulitzer Prize for Poetry. Her fifth collection, *The Book of Men*, was awarded The Paterson Prize. Her fourth book of poems, *Facts About the Moon*, won The Oregon Book Award and was short-listed for the Lenore Marshall Poetry Prize. Laux is also the author of *Awake; What We Carry*, a finalist for the National Book Critic's Circle Award; *Smoke*; as well as a fine small press edition, *The Book of Women*. Visit her online at doriannelaux.net.

Chin-Sun Lee (she/her) is the author of *Upcountry* (debut novel forthcoming with Unnamed Press in fall 2023). Her work has appeared in *The Rumpus, Joyland, The Doctor T.J. Eckleburg Review*, and *The Believer Logger*, among other publications. She's also a contributor to *The New York Times* bestselling anthology *Women in Clothes* (Blue Rider Press/Penguin 2014). A recipient of fellowships from The Hambidge Center, Virginia Center for the Creative Arts, Brush Creek Foundation for the Arts, and the Playa Artist Residency, she earned her MFA in Creative Writing from The New School. More at chinsunlee.com.

Arden Levine's (she/her) debut poetry collection, *Ladies' Abecedary* (Harbor Editions, 2021), was included in CLMP's 2022 Reading List for Women's History Month. Her writing has been featured in *American Life in Poetry* (Poetry Foundation), *Barrow Street, Harvard Review, The Missouri Review*'s Poem-of-the-Week, Poetry Society of America's *Song Cycle* series, WNYC's *Radiolab*, and elsewhere. A New York City municipal employee, Arden's daily work focuses on housing affordability, homelessness prevention, and equitable community development. ardenlevine.com

Kelly McQuain's (he/him) debut poetry collection, *Scrape the Velvet from Your Antlers*, was recently chosen by Texas Review Press for their Southern Breakthrough Series. His chapbook, *Velvet Rodeo*, won the Bloom prize, and his poem "Ruby on Fire" was selected by Dorianne Laux for the inaugural Glitter Bomb Poetry Award. He is a Lambda Fellow and a Sewanee Scholar, and his writing has appeared in *Best New Poets 2020, American Poetry Review, The Pinch, Painted Bride Quarterly, Rogue Agent*, and *Appalachian Review*, as well as such anthologies as *The Queer South*. Also a painter, he lives and works in Philadelphia. KellyMcQuain.wordpress.com.

Katie Manning (she/her) is the founding editor-in-chief of *Whale Road Review* and a professor of writing at Point Loma Nazarene University in San Diego. She is the author of *Tasty Other*, which won the 2016 *Main Street Rag* Poetry Book Award, and her sixth chapbook is *How to Play* (Louisiana Literature Press, 2022). Her poems have appeared in *American Journal of Nursing, december, The Lascaux Review, New Letters*,

Poet Lore, and many other venues, and her poem "What to Expect" was recently featured on the *Poetry Unbound* podcast from The On Being Project. Find her online at katiemanningpoet.com.

Lynn Melnick (she/her) is the author of three poetry collections, including, most recently, *Refusenik*. She is also the author of the memoir *I've Had to Think Up a Way to Survive: On Trauma, Persistence, and Dolly Parton* (University of Texas Press, 2022).

Jenny Molberg (she/her) is the author of three poetry collections: *Marvels of the Invisible* (Tupelo Press, 2017), *Refusal* (LSU Press, 2020), and *The Court of No Record* (forthcoming from LSU Press, 2023). An NEA fellow, her work has recently appeared or is forthcoming in *VIDA, Ploughshares, The Missouri Review, The Rumpus, The Adroit Journal, AGNI, Oprah Quarterly*, and other publications. She is Associate Professor of English and Creative Writing at the University of Central Missouri, where she directs Pleiades Press and edits *Pleiades* magazine. She lives with her dog, Dolly Parton, in Kansas City.

Originally from Tennessee, **Rachel Morgan** (she/her) is the author of the chapbook, *Honey & Blood, Blood & Honey* (Final Thursday Press, 2017) and her work appears in *Crazyhorse, Fence, Prairie Schooner, Denver Quarterly, Salt Hill* and elsewhere. She is the winner of the 2020 Fineline Competition and her work has been nominated for the Best of the Net and a Pushcart Prize. Currently she lives in Iowa, with her dog, Dolly, (named after Dolly Parton) and is the Poetry Editor for the *North American Review*.

Caridad Moro-Gronlier (she/her) is the author of *Tortillera*, winner of the TRP Southern Poetry Breakthrough Prize published by Texas Review Press (2021) and the chapbook *Visionware* (Finishing Line Press, 2009). She is a Contributing Editor for *Grabbed: Poets and Writers Respond to Sexual Assault* (Beacon Press, 2020) and Associate Editor for "SWWIM Every Day," an online daily poetry journal for women identified poets. Recent work can be found in *The Best American Poetry Blog, Verse Daily, Home in Florida: Latinx Writers and the Literature of Uprootedness* (UF Press, 2021), and *Limp Wrist*. She resides in Miami, Florida with her family.

Carolyn Oliver (she/her) is the author of three chapbooks and *Inside the Storm I Want to Touch the Tremble* (University of Utah Press, 2022), winner of the Agha Shahid Ali Prize in Poetry. Carolyn's poems appear in *The Massachusetts Review, Copper Nickel, TAB Journal, Southern Indiana Review, Superstition Review, Shenandoah, Fairy Tale Review, 32 Poems*, and elsewhere. Her awards include the E. E. Cummings Prize from the NEPC, the Goldstein Prize from *Michigan Quarterly Review*, and the Writer's Block Prize in Poetry. Carolyn lives with her family in Massachusetts. Her website is carolynoliver.net.

Dion O'Reilly's (she/they) debut book, *Ghost Dogs*, was shortlisted for a number of prizes including the Catamaran Poetry Prize and The Eric Hoffer Award. Her work appears in *Rattle, The Sun, Cincinnati Review, Narrative*, and *The Slowdown*. Her second book, *Sadness of the Apex Predator*, was chosen for the Portage Poetry Series from University of Wisconsin's Cornerstone Press and will be published in 2024. She frequently hosts The Hive Poetry Collective podcast and facilitates ongoing poetry workshops via Zoom.

Jeffrey Perkins (he/him) earned his BA from Earlham College in Richmond, Indiana and his MA in American Studies from University of Massachusetts Boston. He later studied poetry at Bennington College where he received his MFA and was the recipient of the Jane Kenyon Memorial Scholarship. His poems have been published in *Tupelo Quarterly*, *The Adroit Journal*, *Memorious*, *Rhino*, *The Cortland Review*, *The Massachusetts Review*, and other journals. His first book of poems, *Kingdom*, was released in 2020 by Spork Press. He lives in Vermont.

For **Stephen Roger Powers** (he/him), all it took was one trip to Dollywood in the summer of 1987 when he was thirteen. Dolly's variety show aired on ABC that fall, and his family's VCR was set to record it every week. Stephen has been a Dolly devotee ever since, and nothing makes him happier now than the current Dolly renaissance. He has published three poetry collections with Salmon Poetry, and his short fiction has appeared in several journals. He was an extra in *Joyful Noise*, and he can be seen if you know just where to look.

As a boy, **Steven Reigns** (he/him), with his sister Cindy, would play the VHS of *9-to-5* repeatedly. Holidays were never silent with Dolly Parton's Christmas songs playing in the background. He now lives in Los Angeles and was appointed the first Poet Laureate of West Hollywood. Reigns has lectured and taught writing workshops around the country to LGBT youth and people living with HIV. Currently he is touring The Gay Rub, an exhibition of rubbings from LGBT landmarks. His newest collection *A Quilt for David* (City Lights, 2021) is the product of ten years of research regarding dentist David Acer's life.

Linda Neal Reising (she/her), a member of the Cherokee Nation, grew up in Oklahoma, where she learned to belt out Dolly Parton songs. Published in numerous journals and anthologies, she won the 2012 *Writer's Digest* Competition and has been nominated twice for a Pushcart Prize. Her chapbook, *Re-Writing Family History*, was a finalist for the 2015 Oklahoma Book Award. Reising's first full-length book, *The Keeping*, won the 2020 Kops-Fetherling Book Award. Her second, *Stone Roses*, was a finalist for the Oklahoma Book, as well as the winner of the 2021 Eric Hoffer Award and the Western Heritage Award.

Benjamin Anthony Rhodes (he/him) is a queer and trans poet living in Northeast Ohio. He holds an MFA in Creative Writing from Kent State University and a BA in English from the University of Louisiana at Monroe. On the baritone ukulele, Benjamin can play both "Coat of Many Colors" and "Jolene" (yes, including the iconic finger-picking intro). Check out his work in *Cleveland Review of Books*, *Limp Wrist*, and *Freezeray Poetry*.

Micah Ruelle (she/they) is a queer writer, educator, and editor that resides in Minneapolis. Their work was selected by Kaveh Akbar for Best Poets of 2021. Their chapbook, *Failure to Merge*, was published by Finishing Line Press (2019). You can find their work in *Cultural Daily*, *Chicago Quarterly*, *Cutthroat*, and elsewhere.

Anna Sandy-Elrod (she/her) is a poet, essayist, PhD candidate at Georgia State University, and the editor of joint projects *Birdcoat Quarterly* and Ghost Peach Press. Her work appears or is forthcoming in *Threepenny Review*, *North American Review*,

Green Mountains Review, Iron Horse, Fugue, Pleiades, and others. She currently lives in Amsterdam, the Netherlands with her husband, daughter, cat, and tiny dog. More at annasandyelrod.com.

Roberta Schultz (she/her) is a singer songwriter, teacher and poet originally from Grant's Lick, KY. Her poems and song lyrics have appeared in *Women Speak, Vol.7, Sheila-Na-Gig, Panoplyzine, Riparian, Pine Mountain Sand & Gravel, Kakalak* and other anthologies. Three of her chapbooks, *Outposts on the Border of Longing, Songs from the Shaper's Harp,* and *Touchstones* were published by Finishing Line Press. Her latest chapbook of poetry, *Asking Price,* was accepted by Workhorse Writers for their 2022 series. *Underscore,* 2022, from Dos Madres Press, is her first full-length collection.

Maureen Seaton (she/her) has authored twenty-five poetry collections, both solo and collaborative–recently, *Undersea* (Jackleg, 2021); *Myth America* (Anhinga, 2020), a collaborative collection with Carolina Hospital, Nicole Hospital-Medina, and Holly Iglesias; and *Sweet World* (CavanKerry, 2019), winner of the Florida Book Award. Poetry honors include the Lambda Literary Award, NEA, and Pushcart. A memoir, *Sex Talks to Girls* (Wisconsin, 2008, 2018), also garnered a Lammy. With Denise Duhamel and David Trinidad, she co-edited *Saints of Hysteria: A Half-Century of Collaborative American Poetry* (Soft Skull); and with Neil de la Flor, she co-edited *Reading Queer: Poetry in a Time of Chaos* (Anhinga).

Gregg Shapiro (he/him) is the author of six books of poetry and two short story collections, including *Fear of Muses* (Souvenir Spoon Books, 2022) and *How to Whistle* (Rattling Good Yarns Press, 2021). An entertainment journalist whose interviews and reviews run in a variety of regional LGBTQ+ outlets, Shapiro lives in South Florida with his husband, writer Rick Karlin, and their diva dog Coco.

L.J. Sysko (she/her) is the author of *The Daughter of Man* (2023 Miller Williams Poetry Series, University of Arkansas Press) and *Battledore* (New Women's Voices Chapbook Series, Finishing Line Press, 2017). Her work has appeared in *Ploughshares, The Missouri Review*'s "Poem of The Week," Best New Poets, and elsewhere. She holds a B.A. from Lafayette College and an M.F.A. from New England College. She writes for the President of Delaware State University and resides in Wilmington, Delaware with her family.

Nicole Tallman (she/her) is a poet, ghostwriter, and editor living in Miami. She is the author of three collections: *Something Kindred* (The Southern Collective Experience Press, 2022), *Poems for the People* (The Southern Collective Experience Press, 2023) and *Fersace* (Redacted Books, 2023). She also serves as the Poetry Ambassador for Miami-Dade County, Poetry and Interviews Editor for *The Blue Mountain Review,* and Associate Editor for *South Florida Poetry Journal.* Find her on Twitter and Instagram @natallman and online at nicoletallman.com.

Kerry Trautman (she/her) is a lifelong Ohioan whose work has appeared in dozens of anthologies and journals. Her first Dolly memory was a dance recital where teenage girls performed to "A Lil' Ole Bitty Pissant Country Place," and backstage, age seven, she sensed it was delightfully naughty, but didn't know why. Kerry's books are, *Things*

That Come in Boxes (Kingcraft Press 2012), *To Have Hoped* (Finishing Line Press 2015), *Artifacts* (NightBallet Press 2017), *To be Nonchalantly Alive* (Kelsay Books 2020), and *Marilyn: Self-Portrait, Oil on Canvas* (Gutter Snob Books 2022). Her next full-length collection is forthcoming from Roadside Press.

Rosemerry Wahtola Trommer (she/her) co-hosts the *Emerging Form* podcast on creative process, Secret Agents of Change (a surreptitious kindness cabal), and Soul Writer's Circle. Her poetry has appeared on *A Prairie Home Companion, PBS News Hour, O Magazine, American Life in Poetry,* on the Carnegie Hall stage, and on river rocks she leaves around town. Since 2006, she's written a poem a day. Her collection *Hush* won the Halcyon Prize. *Naked for Tea* was a finalist for the Able Muse Book Award. Her next collection, *All the Honey,* comes out in April, 2023. One-word mantra: Adjust.

Dan Vera (he/him) is a first-gen, borderlands born Queer-Tejano Latinx writer, editor, and literary historian of Cuban/Caribbean ancestry. Awarded the Oscar Wilde Award for Poetry and the Letras Latinas/Red Hen Poetry Prize, he co-edited *Imaniman: Poets Writing In The Anzaldúan Borderlands* and authored two books of poetry. He's been featured by the Poetry Foundation, the NEA and in academic curricula, various journals and anthologies. He lives in Washington, DC with his beloved Pete and their blessed dog Blossom.

Isaiah Vianese (he/him) is author of the poetry collection, *Men and Music* (Coyote Creek Books 2016). His poems have appeared in *Assaracus, Divot, Impossible Archetype, Limp Wrist, Moon City Review,* and *Rise Up Review,* among others. He is also author of the chapbook, *Stopping on the Old Highway* (Recycled Karma Press 2009). He lives in New York City.

Donna Vorreyer (she/her) is the author of *To Everything There Is* (2020), *Every Love Story is an Apocalypse Story* (2016) and *A House of Many Windows* (2013), all from Sundress Publications. An associate editor for *Rhino Poetry,* she hosts the monthly online reading series *A Hundred Pitchers of Honey.*

Julie Marie Wade (she/her) teaches in the creative writing program at Florida International University in Miami. She is the author of many collections of poetry, prose, and hybrid forms, including, most recently *Skirted: Poems* (The Word Works, 2021) and *Just an Ordinary Woman Breathing* (The Ohio State University Press, 2020).

Yvonne Zipter (she/her) is the author of the poetry collections *The Wordless Lullaby of Crickets* (forthcoming, 2023), *Kissing the Long Face of the Greyhound, The Patience of Metal,* and *Like Some Bookie God.* Her published poems are currently being sold individually in Chicago in two repurposed toy-vending machines, the proceeds of which are donated to the nonprofit arts organization Arts Alive Chicago. She is also the author of the nonfiction books *Diamonds Are a Dyke's Best Friend* and *Ransacking the Closet,* and the Russian historical novel *Infraction.*

MURALIST / PHOTOGRAPHER BIOS

Travis Collinsworth (he/him) is co-owner of The 5 Spot. Visit them online at the5spot. club. Photograph: *Dolly at The 5 Spot* (back cover, center).

Catherine Cowan Compton (she/her) currently lives in Nashville where her family has resided for generations. A lifelong Dolly fan, she grew up singing along to Dolly tunes while painting furniture, doing renovations, and taking on various arts and crafts projects. She continues to be inspired by how Dolly's music endures in times of both challenge and celebration. To her, Dolly will always be the queen of country music. Photograph: *Dolly at Hume-Fogg High School* (back cover, right).

Matt Fitt (he/him) has over 15 years of experience as a professional photographer. His work has appeared in numerous publications including the *San Francisco Chronicle* and *East Bay Express*. He has worked with politically progressive candidates and politicians on multiple campaigns, and with organizations that promote social and ecological justice. Visit him online at mattfitt.com. Photograph: *Dolly at Strut Bar & Club* (back cover, top).

David Gilmore (he/him) has a paint-on-everything approach to art making. That everything includes: walls, canvas, furniture, accessories, surfboards, and even bodies. Whatever the surface, his intention is to create something compelling and thought-provoking. Visit him online at davidgilmorestudio.com. Mural: *Dolly at Strut Bar & Club* (back cover, top).

Michelle Lytle (she/her) has been a wedding photographer for over 15 years. When she moved into the property with her wife, Robyn, in 2017, they added the Dolly mural to the front fence to shine out over the neighborhood and welcome wedding couples as they arrived at the event space. Since then it has become a community landmark. Visit her online at michellelytle.com. Mural & Photograph: *Dolly at the Lytle House* (back cover, left).

Kim Radford (she/her) is a Tennessee-based painter and muralist. A graduate of Austin Peay State University, she is known for spotlighting women artists in her work—including Joni Mitchell, Lilly Hyatt, Amanda Shires, Brandi Carlisle, Allison Russell, and Valerie June. She has also painted a number of Dolly Parton murals in Tennessee and Georgia. Visit her online at kimradfordart.com. Murals: *Dolly at The 5 Spot* (back cover, center) and *Dolly at Hume-Fogg High School* (back cover, right).

EDITOR BIOS

Julie E. Bloemeke (she/her) is the 2021 Georgia Author of the Year Finalist for Poetry. Her debut full-length collection *Slide to Unlock* (Sibling Rivalry Press, 2020) was also chosen as a 2021 Book All Georgians Should Read. Winner of the 2022 *Third Coast Poetry Prize* and a finalist for the 2020 Fischer Poetry Prize, her work has appeared in numerous anthologies and publications including *Writer's Chronicle, Prairie Schooner, Nimrod, Gulf Coast, EcoTheo Review,* and others. Co-editor for the Dolly Parton tribute issue of *Limp Wrist,* an associate editor for *South Carolina Review,* and a Virginia Center for the Creative Arts fellow, she is also a freelance writer and editor. She holds her MA in American Literature from the University of South Carolina and her MFA in poetry from the Bennington Writing Seminars. A proud native of Toledo, she currently lives in Atlanta. Visit her online at jebloemeke.com.

Julie has yet to make a pilgrimage to Pigeon Forge. She knows that when she finally does, it will be poetry that leads her to Dolly Parton.

Dustin Brookshire (he/him), a finalist for the 2021 Scotti Merrill Award, is the curator of the Wild & Precious Life Series, editor of *Limp Wrist,* and program director for Reading Queer. He is the author of three chapbooks—*Never Picked First For Playtime* (Harbor Editions, 2023), *Love Most Of You Too* (Harbor Editions, 2021) and *To The One Who Raped Me* (Sibling Rivalry Press, 2012). His work has earned him both a Pushcart and Best of the Net nomination and been anthologized and published in numerous journals. Visit him online at dustinbrookshire.com.

Dustin looks forward to being the person that takes Julie to her first Pigeon Forge visit, and he can't wait to spend an entire day with her at Dollywood.

Editors Dustin Brookshire and Julie E. Bloemeke, August 4, 2011, on the
Alpharetta, GA stop of Dolly's *Better Day* tour.
(Photograph by Rob Warrington)